USING TECHNOLOGY IN MIDDLE GRADES LANGUAGE ARTS

Strategies to Improve Student Learning

Katrina Hunter-Mintz

Rowman & Littlefield Education
Lanham, Maryland • Toronto • Plymouth, UK
2008

Published in the United States of America
by Rowman & Littlefield Education
A Division of Rowman & Littlefield Publishers, Inc.
A wholly owned subsidary of The Rowman & Littlefield Publishing
Group, Inc.
4501 Forbes Boulevard, Suite 200, Lanham, Maryland 20706
www.rowmaneducation.com

Estover Road
Plymouth PL6 7PY
United Kingdom

British Library Cataloguing in Publication Information Available

Library of Congress Cataloging-in-Publication Data

Hunter-Mintz, Katrina, 1969–
    Using technology in middle grades language arts : strategies to
improve student learning / Katrina Hunter-Mintz.
        p. cm.
    Includes bibliographical references.
    ISBN-13: 978-1-57886-792-9 (hardcover : alk. paper)
    ISBN-13: 978-1-57886-793-6 (pbk. : alk. paper)
    ISBN-10: 1-57886-792-4 (hardcover : alk. paper)
    ISBN-10: 1-57886-793-2 (pbk. : alk. paper)
    1. Language arts (Middle school)—Computer-assisted instruction.
    I. Title.
    LB1631.3.H86 2008
    428.0071'2—dc22   2007048798

CONTENTS

❶

INTRODUCTION

☀ FOCUS QUESTIONS

- What impact has technology had on social interactions and language development in your classroom? In your personal experience?
- What are your beliefs about the social contexts of learning?
- How has the impact of technology broadened our literate society through both the World Wide Web and growing cultural diversity?

Let me offer you a ticket for passage into my favorite community of learners. We will be departing from almost any location on earth. If we have wireless capabilities and a laptop, we can, like Harry Potter, enter this community through any portal from any train station, airport, or classroom. Upon arrival you will notice that multiple languages are spoken here, and that ideas are accepted and shared globally. There are no boundaries, limits, or walls. The impossible is only a few weeks away and the ideas that abound here are ever evolving.

After 12 years of teaching in a classroom with walls and feeling a little trapped now and then, I discovered a community of learners where I am free to explore a vast array of new information using so many different technologies. Not only are there no boundaries as far as the amount and type of information I can find here, but there are infinite technology tools that allow me to express or communicate my new knowledge to my students in unique ways.

Teaching is my first and only career choice. I began teaching high school English and drama a mere 17 days after completing my bachelor's degree, and haven't stopped since that day. I remember that first year of late nights writing out lesson plans on a legal pad and then typing them on my Radio Shack TRS80, my first computer. I believe they have those in museums now. As I continued to teach, I embraced technology gracefully. I did not kick and scream when I was first asked to complete my lesson plans on the one computer in my classroom, or when I was trained to use administrative software to grade students, keep permanent records, and record disciplinary actions. I never complained when my single classroom computer failed to function properly and the technical service guys were running days behind. No, I simply disassembled the whole thing myself and determined quickly that I should stick to using the computer for educational purposes rather than attempting to fix it when it wasn't following my commands.

As a teacher of language arts there was no more powerful tool for me than the pen, until I learned to compose with a keyboard rather than pen and paper. I do realize that the move from pen and paper to the keyboard and cyberspace is more difficult for some students and teachers. I believe, however, that technology has changed the definition of literacy during the past two decades, and that those who fail to address these changes will fall further and further behind. As I continued my own education through a master's degree program, an educational specialist program, and finally a doctoral program, I continued to find new ways to implement technology in my own language arts classroom. I could see my students embracing new methods for communication, and I certainly did not want to be left behind. I have taken multiple online courses for fun, for professional development, and for graduate credit. While working on my doctoral degree, I was asked to write an online course for the state's online high school. I surveyed the students in my traditional classroom, spoke with fellow participants in a course I was taking, and participated in an online discussion group in order to better understand the possibility of distance education in high schools. At first I was a little scared of being replaced by a computer! I was the teacher. I needed to see those students' faces, read their body language, and develop a relationship that allowed me to make decisions about instructional methods. No computer could do that!

It took me very little time to realize that educational technology would never replace teachers. It is one of the most powerful instructional tools I have ever used. It motivates students when little else will. Best of all, the tools of technology allow my students to be active and successful participants in an ever-growing and ever-changing community of learners. They will be better prepared for the workplace, better prepared to compete for scholarships and jobs, and better prepared to communicate with other technologically literate members of this new community.

As you read this book, it is my hope that you too will realize the potential for new technologies in your classrooms. You will find information in this book that helps you reflect on your own beliefs about teaching and learning and how technology can enhance your students' learning. This book will offer you some points upon which to reflect. Any adjustments, additions, or implementations we make with respect to our teaching practices should be viewed through our own individual lenses. Each classroom is different. Each teacher is unique. All students are individuals with distinctive talents, behaviors, and learning characteristics. Therefore, it is important that we first share who we are as teachers and what we believe about the teaching–learning process.

This text also asks you to think about your methods for designing learning activities. By the time you finish this book, you will be able to articulate your beliefs about the integration of technology into your view of learning. You will adjust or enhance your instructional design method so that you identify and select appropriate support technologies. It is my hope that when you finish this book, you will have improved skill in using a word processor, presentation software, and the Internet; in integrating electronic portfolios; and in utilizing WebQuests. In improving these skills and exploring the Internet, you will compile a collection of lesson plans for use in your classroom and have an opportunity to build your own WebQuest and your own plan for implementing an electronic portfolio.

CREATING COMMUNITIES OF LITERATE LEARNERS

There are a few principles we can apply to any classroom where *social constructivism* is practiced. So, first of all, what is social constructivism? Constructivism is one of many learning theories that explain what occurs in our minds as we learn. This particular learning theory posits that learning is promoted through collaboration among students and teachers alike. Our students share background knowledge and learn content through negotiation that takes place within a community of learners. Scholars and researchers in the field of reading refer to these phenomena as the hermeneutic circle (Gadamer, 1975).

Technology has pushed the boundaries of this community of learners without ceasing during the last few decades. We and our students now have immediate access to world news and events, the latest entertainment, and a vast compilation of new information. To our students who have access to this technology, the community in which we learn is boundless, the knowledge found there is all-embracing, and the uses for these tools are multiple.

It is important that we strive to create a community of literate learners in our language arts classrooms, by implementing activities and information that make use of these new technologies and that provide students with a manner in which to measure the value of information found in their global community of learners. In order to implement technology in our classrooms successfully, we, as teachers, must determine how technology will fit into our own teaching–learning model. This means taking a few minutes to examine what we believe about the community of learners in our classrooms, how our individual students learn and participate in the communication cycle, and how we ourselves plan, implement, and teach.

In first examining our beliefs about teaching, learning, and the role of technology, it is good to acknowledge that diverse learning theories provide our foundation for understanding the teaching–learning process. Each of us has possibly read about many of these theories, reflected on our teaching practice, and adjusted our teaching so that we reveal our own eclectic view of learning theory. One umbrella under which many learning theories fall is social constructivism. Knowing a few basic principles of social constructivist classrooms will help us better understand how the proper use of technology tools will help to bring about higher levels of critical and creative thinking among our students.

The first principle states that learning and development are social and collaborative activities. This emphasizes the crucial need to provide students time to interact with their peers and their teachers. This principle suggests that using technology to enhance communication, contact, and interaction is beneficial. Since students construct understanding and meaning for themselves, it is not enough to simply provide information through these new technologies. We must provide students with activities and technological tools that facilitate their construction of new knowledge. Figure 1.1 illustrates the elements essential to successful integration of technology into the language arts curriculum.

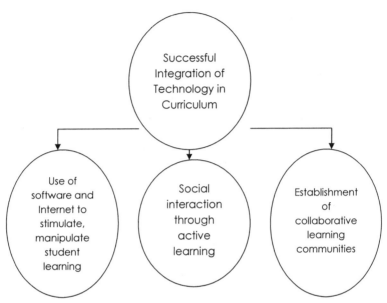

Figure 1.1.   The elements essential to successful integration of technology into the language arts curriculum.

THE INFLUENCE OF LEV VYGOTSKY

If we believe that students are not empty tablets upon which teachers write, but rather that students come to us with a basic process for learning new material already in place, then it is important to determine how we can present information and provide students with strategies for learning. This is the second principle of social constructivism. Students learn in different ways at different levels. Lev Vygotsky called the level of optimum learning the *zone of proximal development* (ZPD). Simply put, this means that students learn best when the information presented and the strategies to be used are neither *frustrational* (too far above what the student can understand without support from the teacher) nor *independent* (too easy for the student to master with no support from the teacher). The student's ZPD is the level for optimum learning.

Instruction at this level asks the student to build on knowledge already in place, but is such that the student needs appropriate support and guidance from the teacher or peers. It is simple to say that technology is useful in a language arts classroom because it opens the doors to new information. It is more difficult to know how to use technology to teach students to think. Since more is not necessarily better, having students surf the Internet because more information can be found there is not necessarily a successful use of technology. Implementing technology tools may require that you adjust the method you currently use for planning instruction. A common instructional design method has teachers consider the characteristics of the learners, articulate objectives, establish the learning environment, identify teaching and learning strategies, identify and select support materials, and evaluate and revise the lesson.

Teachers who implement technological tools may need to place extra emphasis on identifying and selecting support materials and technologies. There are so many free teacher tools on the Internet. How do we know which ones are worth the investment in time we must make in order to use them properly? We invest the time in exploration and evaluation. It is difficult to keep up with the fast pace at which new technologies are introduced to education. While implementing technology in your classroom, it will be beneficial to read publications, either electronic or print, that evaluate new software, hardware, and Internet sites for teachers. You will find some of these sites listed in the Resources section of this book.

The third principle of social constructivism recommends that school learning occur in a meaningful context and relate out-of-school experiences to the students' school experiences. Technology directly assists teachers in areas of extreme importance in relation to this principle. While our learning environments are growing and changing, so too are our students' characteristics. We are becoming a nation of great diversity: diversity of race and ethnicity, diversity of language, diversity of socioeconomic class, diversity of gender, and diversity of special needs. In planning to use, and to teach students to use, the tools of technology, you will be addressing each of these diversity issues in various ways.

There is an abundance of assistive technology for students with special needs. Take some time while reading this book to search the Web for suggestions and lesson plans that specifically address the needs of these students in our classrooms. If you happen to teach students whose native language is not English, the Internet offers many helpful resources. Online you will find translators, language dictionaries, and many other technology tools for supporting the linguistic development of these language learners. By integrating technology tools into your language arts instruction, you can easily build your cultural awareness and the cultural awareness of your students, learn about other cultures in your school, and assist students of culturally diverse backgrounds in finding positive role models.

Multiliteracy is a new term surfacing in much of the research on literacy development. It simply means that it is no longer sufficient to think of literate individuals as those who are able to read and write. We now need multiple literacies such as visual literacy, media literacy, and digital literacy. The manner in which we as teachers and adults use these new types of literacies may be much different from the ways our students use them.

For example, some adults did not grow up with video games as entertainment. When did you first read an entire e-book online? Have you ever chatted on Instant Messenger and completed research for a term paper simultaneously? Adolescents have developed some very complex multitasking skills that employ technology. For some middle school and high school students, the use of a computer at home is very different from the purposes and uses of a computer at school. As teachers attempting to enhance the language arts curriculum by integrating technological tools, we must provide a meaningful context for our instruction and attempt to relate it to our students' multiliteracies. Our explorations and activities in this book will help us accomplish this goal.

TECHNOLOGY TOOLS AND THE STANDARDS

Throughout this book *technology tools* are mentioned. What are technology tools? Since tools are generally objects that help us do work, we can think of technology tools as objects, machines, software, and so forth that we use to help us accomplish our educational goals. Some common examples of tools for productivity and professional practice are word processing, Internet and e-mail, curriculum software, CD-ROM encyclopedias, and digital imaging. These tools are ineffective unless we know how to use them properly. As teachers, we need to be able to use these tools ourselves and teach our students to use these tools. In implementing technology tools in our language arts classrooms, we will meet three sets of standards and address the standards of the National Board for Professional Teaching Standards (NBPTS) for early adolescence/English language arts (EALA).

The International Society for Technology in Education (ISTE) developed two sets of standards concerning the implementation of technology for classroom instruction. The first set of standards is for students. These standards cover six broad topics: (1) basic operations and concepts; (2) social, ethical, and human issues; (3) technology productivity tools; (4) technology and communications tools; (5) technology research tools; and (6) technology problem-solving and decision-making tools.

The second set of standards is geared toward teachers and includes six broad topics: (1) technology operations and concepts; (2) planning and designing learning environments and experiences; (3) teaching, learning, and the curriculum; (4) assessment and evaluation; (5) productivity and professional practice; and (6) social, ethical, legal, and human issues.

In completing the activities found in this text you will meet some of the standards for ISTE's National Educational Technology Standards (NETS) for Teachers and be prepared to address ISTE's NETS for students. You may find it useful to visit ISTE's website and become familiar with both sets of standards.

The National Council of Teachers of English (NCTE) and the International Reading Association, both organizations devoted to improving the teaching and learning of English and the language arts, have developed 12 standards for language arts. Several of these standards provide specific references to technology. Through completing the activities within this text you will compile a collection of lesson plans that address standards 1, 3, 6, 7, and 8. It will be useful for you to visit the NCTE website to familiarize yourself with these standards. After viewing both sets of standards, you should be able to make clear connections between the technology standards and the language arts standards.

NBPTS is a nonprofit, nonpartisan organization founded in 1987 and committed to basic reform in education. It recognizes that teaching is at the heart of education, and offers teacher certification to candidates who successfully complete the rigorous certification process. The basis of this certification is a set of standards for each certificate offered. In the field of English/language arts, NBPTS offers certificates in early- and middle-childhood literacy, reading and language arts, early adolescence/English language arts, and adolescence and young adulthood/English language arts. These certificates are built around common standards. These standards are divided into three major sections: (1) Preparing the Way for Productive Student Learning, (2) Advancing Student Learning in the Classroom, and (3) Supporting Student Learning through Long-Range Initiatives. The information and activities in this book focus on the following NBPTS/EALA standards:

I. Knowledge of Students
III. Engagement
IV. Learning Environment
VIII. Reading
IX. Writing
X. Listening, Speaking and Viewing

XIV. Self-Reflection

XV. Professional Community

Each chapter provides a reference to specific standards and how those standards may be met through activities suggested within the chapters.

SUMMARY

In this chapter we have reflected on our knowledge of learning theories and our experiences in our classrooms in order to review our beliefs about the teaching–learning process. These beliefs impact our actions as teachers in defining and forming a community of literate learners. As we teach and implement new elements in our teaching practice, we hone our skills and adjust our beliefs. Throughout this text it will be beneficial to reflect on what you have learned, and to synthesize your view of how your students learn best and how you can best communicate with them; how to adapt your teaching style and new technologies to your students' needs; and how educational technology fits into your synthesized view of teaching and learning.

As we add technology tools and skills, keep in mind that you are addressing three sets of national standards: ISTE NETS for teachers and students, NCTE's English Language Arts standards, and NBPTS EALA standards. These standards provide accountability in our practice. In meeting these standards through the implementation of technology tools, we are also addressing diversity among our students and providing our students with social and collaborative activities that enhance their language and literacy development.

Instructional design can be a little different when we begin to choose the technological tools that address the needs of a particular lesson or activity. As you explore the Internet, software, and lesson plans, keep in mind that you should continually evaluate the usefulness of these tools. It may be a good idea to keep a list of Internet sites that you found particularly easy to use or useful for a particular topic in language arts. Be cautious of using every lesson from the Internet exactly as you find it. You know your students and their abilities better than anyone. You also know your habits, strengths, and weaknesses as a teacher. Adjust instructional ideas you find online to fit your classroom, your students, and your practice. If you are reading this book as part of a book study group, you may want to share your ideas with members of that particular learning community. Educators learn best from the experience of fellow educators.

REFERENCE

Gadamer, H. (1975). *Truth and method* (Sheed and Ward Ltd., Trans.). New York: Seabury Press.

2

ENHANCING ACTIVE LEARNING WITH TECHNOLOGY

FOCUS QUESTIONS

- How are you currently using online lesson plans that include active learning with technology?
- How do you teach your students strategic reading and thinking?
- To what extent are you aware of your own use of strategies used by proficient readers: drawing inferences, visualizing, determining important ideas, and synthesizing information?

Think back to the best lesson you've taught thus far in your teaching career. Did you achieve the learning outcomes you wanted to achieve? Did you enjoy teaching the lesson? Did your students enjoy learning the material? Even if the concepts were a little difficult, were the students engaged in learning the material? If you answered yes to any of these questions, there's a good chance you incorporated *active learning* into your lesson. Active learning is considered to be one of the most important principles of good teaching practice. What is active learning? It's more than a collection of activities.

Active learning is an attitude of both teacher and students that makes learning more effective. It means to be engaged, mentally, physically, or emotionally, in learning a concept. The true purpose of active learning strategies is to form lifelong habits regarding how you think, what you learn, and why you are learning. Active learning encourages students to take responsibility for their own education.

Remember in the previous chapter when you reflected on what you believed about learning? Was there an element of action involved in your belief? If you've only recently begun to incorporate technology into your lessons, it's easy to get caught up in the wave of including technology for technology's sake. The purpose of technology should always be to enhance learning. If the successful lessons you've taught without technology included active learning activities, then you'll probably be more apt to seek out lesson plans that include those same types of activities.

Employing technology for technology's sake undermines the effective teaching and learning that can result from the proper use of technology as an educational tool. Remember in the previous chapter when I explained that at first I was uneasy with online courses because I feared that computers might someday become advanced enough to "teach" without the presence of teachers? So, do computers do a better job of helping teachers teach content than traditional methods? Years of research and experience have taught us the predictable outcomes of most traditional methods for teaching language arts. Technology in education is relatively new and constantly changing. We are just beginning to see predictable outcomes. Often the first vision we have of technology in language arts encompasses presentation devices such as multimedia and the Internet. These can deliver information in a format that is more interesting to our students.

If, as teachers, we simply deliver information, do our students necessarily learn the new information? No. Technology does offer information in a dynamic and more appealing format, but it does not teach students to use the complicated process of building new knowledge, understanding, and use of information. We must teach students to use technology in our language arts classes, to facilitate their own learning. We do this by ensuring that where there is technology in our lessons, there is also meaningful activity and engagement.

Teachers can employ their knowledge of Bloom's Taxonomy (figure 2.1) when structuring any lesson, but it is particularly useful when implementing technology. All of the principles of good

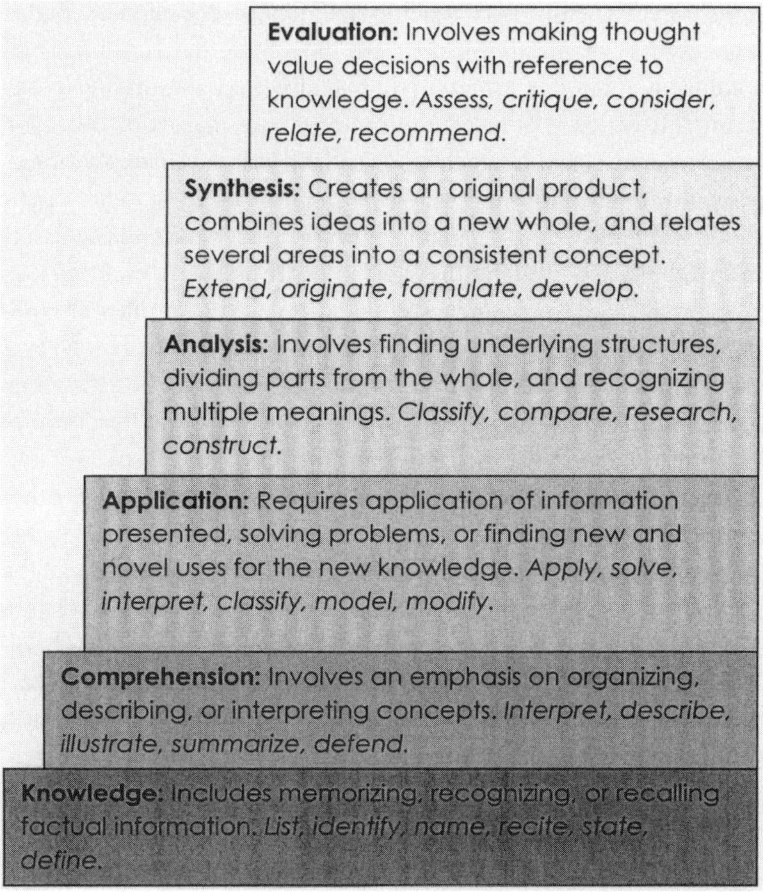

Evaluation: Involves making thought value decisions with reference to knowledge. *Assess, critique, consider, relate, recommend.*

Synthesis: Creates an original product, combines ideas into a new whole, and relates several areas into a consistent concept. *Extend, originate, formulate, develop.*

Analysis: Involves finding underlying structures, dividing parts from the whole, and recognizing multiple meanings. *Classify, compare, research, construct.*

Application: Requires application of information presented, solving problems, or finding new and novel uses for the new knowledge. *Apply, solve, interpret, classify, model, modify.*

Comprehension: Involves an emphasis on organizing, describing, or interpreting concepts. *Interpret, describe, illustrate, summarize, defend.*

Knowledge: Includes memorizing, recognizing, or recalling factual information. *List, identify, name, recite, state, define.*

Figure 2.1. Taxonomy by Bloom.

teaching should remain important when we incorporate technology. Remember to use the action words related to each level of the taxonomy. This taxonomy describes levels of cognition. We have described it, defined it, and reinforced the idea, but what does this look like in our classrooms? It can be a little loud. It may seem a little chaotic at times. I may very well require that students discuss the information provided in the form of software, electronic text, or websites.

Have you ever found yourself wishing that your students would come to class with every reading assignment completed? Better yet, how would you feel if they not only came to class having all reading assignments completed, but also had something to say about the reading! What if they offered summaries of the main ideas, or analyses of characters, or reflections on personal connections they made with the text? Wouldn't it be exciting to hear their ideas? Students who are capable of these actions possess the habits and strategies of proficient readers and writers.

So how do we teach those students who are not proficient readers and writers? We get them actively involved with the text. It may be that these students are better suited to begin with visual learning. Visualizing and inferring are two strategies that require learners to be actively involved. They do not occur in isolation, but rather interweave. Inferring occurs at the junction of a few other active learning strategies: questioning, connecting, and engaging the text. When technology is used, these strategies become the catalyst for changing information delivered by the computer into knowledge understood and used by the student. You see, technology alone cannot simply increase anyone's knowledge. It is a tool that delivers information, in somewhat the same manner that a textbook delivers information. Until teachers add the magical element of active learning, students gain very little from the delivery of information.

Because the computer offers audio, video, and printed text, it is the perfect context for teaching students to become actively involved in learning by using strategies such as visualizing and inferring. Graphic organizers can assist students in organizing information visually and making connections among elements or concepts. While students can be actively involved in completing a teacher-generated graphic organizer, think how much more critically they must think in order to create the organizer themselves. Please see the Suggested Reading section for this chapter to read more about graphic organizers.

There are many other teaching methods and lesson-design methods that ensure students are engaged in the content. Keep in mind that these methods are just as valuable to you when you begin to implement technology as they are when your instruction doesn't involve technology. You may find it useful to learn more about problem-based instruction. Problem-based instruction has been interpreted at many levels. For the classroom teacher, problem-based learning usually means that the lesson presents the students with a particular problem, and then, through group work, research, discussion, and trial and error, students propose solutions to the problem. This method of instruction can be simple or very complex.

Teachers can present problems that are not easily solvable or that may not have only one correct solution, and often they can present problems that require that students exercise higher levels of thinking to propose a solution. You'll find more information on problem-based learning and its close relative, inquiry-based instruction, in the Resources section of this text.

Type "lesson plan" into the search section of any search engine, and you are likely to generate more than 1,000 hits. Lesson plan sites are endless on the Internet. Unfortunately, with the explosion of information comes the responsibility to evaluate the information before using it. In other words, you probably shouldn't use just any lesson plan found on the Internet. Anyone can create a website and list lesson plans. You should always search for credible websites that review lesson plans before posting them to the Internet.

In evaluating websites for lesson plans, you may consider the following set of questions:

- Is the site credible and reliable? Is it published by an educational organization?
- Are the lessons aligned with standards (International Society for Technology in Education [ISTE] standards, National Council of Teachers of English [NCTE]/International Reading Association [IRA] Language Arts standards, or state standards)?
- Are the lesson plans reviewed by teachers or other educational professionals before being published to the Web?
- Is the lesson plan format complete? Does it consider the learning styles of students? Does it offer accommodations for English to Speakers of Other Languages [ESOL], special needs, and diverse students?

One of the most useful sites I've found in language arts instruction is ReadWriteThink.org. This site is maintained by the IRA and the NCTE. Lessons found here are reviewed by classroom teachers and others in the education profession and must be based upon solid, research-proven theories. When looking for a reliable source for lesson plans, you may want to begin with professional organizations in education or the language arts content area. In the Resources section of this text, I've listed some reliable sites that may be helpful to you.

When you locate a reliable source, it is a good idea to save the site to your list of favorites. This list will make your use of the Internet for lesson plans more efficient. You create a list of favorites by opening your Web browser (e.g., Internet Explorer, Netscape, Firefox, Safari) and going to the site you've chosen, by searching for the site or typing the address into the address area just below the toolbar. Click on the tab labeled "favorites" along the top of the toolbar. A drop-down menu appears. Find and click on "add to favorites." A new dialog box appears, showing you a list of folders.

If you would like to create a folder for your favorite lesson plan site, click on "new folder," give the folder a name, and click "ok." The "new folder" dialog box disappears, and you return to your "add to favorites" dialog box. The folder you created should now be highlighted. Click "ok" to add the site to your new folder. Each time you want to visit your favorite lesson plan sites, simply open your browser and click on the "favorites" tab on the top toolbar, and your saved favorites will appear in the drop-down menu.

As part of your assignment for this chapter, you'll be asked to download a 30-day trial of Inspiration software. This software is used for creating graphic organizers, a strategy discussed earlier in this chapter. Please see the Resources section of this text for the Web address for this site. You'll also find step-by-step directions for using a template in Inspiration at the Baylor site listed in the Resources section of this text. This site offers step-by-step guides for using all of the language arts templates included in the Inspiration software.

In learning about integrating technology into your language arts curriculum, we have seen that technology is a tool for enhancing teaching and learning. Technology cannot replace good teaching or good teachers. As you read the remaining chapters in this book, keep in mind that you are simply learning to enhance your own teaching practice and that, by doing so, you'll enhance the success of your students in reaching their learning goals.

When searching for lesson plans online, remember to evaluate the website that publishes the plans. Use the guidelines presented in chapter 4 to evaluate the lessons. It is also important to remember that you know your students and your objectives better than the author of any lesson plan. Be sure the lesson plan can easily be modified for optimum teaching and learning in your classroom. Make any necessary adjustments, implement the lesson, and then follow through by evaluating the outcomes. Think reflectively about the successes and failures of the lesson. Don't give up on the first try! As with any new method, technology integration takes time; practice; the devising of solutions to weaknesses; and persistence in reaching success.

It is important to avoid implementing technology for technology's sake. Lessons involving technology should require students to become actively engaged in the content. As we all know, learning is not passive, and students are not blank pages on which teachers write information. Abundant information is not knowledge. Knowledge is information put to use in novel and critical ways. Select and adjust lessons so that they require students to engage in all levels of Bloom's Taxonomy. Focus lessons with technology on multiple levels of this cognitive hierarchy, and teach students to use technology to improve their thinking skills rather than using computers to gather information.

When trying out new software, such as Inspiration, you'll need to learn how to use the software and then teach your students to use the software to enhance their own learning. In doing this, you are meeting both the ISTE standards for teachers (by using the software yourself) and the ISTE standards for students (by having students use the software to enhance their own learning). For more information about the standards for language arts and technology, please feel free to take a look back at chapter 1.

If you are reading this book as part of a book study in a learning community, you may want to complete the following activity:

Think of a lesson plan you've taught in the past that could use a little technological spice, or a new lesson plan you may have found in your Internet searching. Rewrite the lesson plan so that it incorporates a student-generated graphic organizer. Download a free 30-day trial of Inspiration at www.inspiration.com/productinfo/inspirationpalmos/index.cfm. Following the step-by-step instructions for using a template found at www.baylor.edu/Electronic Library/support/documentation/inspiration/TemplateGuide.pdf, create a graphic organizer for use as an example for your students as you teach the lesson. When you've completed the lesson plan and the example graphic organizer, share your ideas for extensions and elaborations with the members of your learning community.

USING TEMPLATES IN INSPIRATION

1. In order to open a template, go to the "file" menu and click on "open template." This is the first type of template you may use in Inspiration.
2. Select the appropriate template, and click on the template to open it.
3. There are *customized templates* that you may choose to use as a starting point for a particular project.
4. After you have finished your document, find the utility window at the top and select "template wizard." This allows you to create your own template for multiple uses.
5. Once you've selected this option, you will be prompted through a series of steps to create your new template.
6. This wizard establishes how a document will open in a screen. You may change the symbols, links, fonts, and so on.
7. When you save your newly created template, Inspiration automatically opens the Inspiration template folder; but you may choose to save your document in other places. You may choose to save the file on a server for easy student access.

3

USING TECHNOLOGY TO RESPOND TO LITERATURE

☀ FOCUS QUESTIONS

- How often do you explore online digital libraries and collections of online literature selections?
- What possibilities do you believe exist for online books?
- Is there a difference in the reading process when students read online texts as opposed to printed text?
- How often do you or your students participate as members of interpretive communities, exploring and evaluating multimedia critiques of literature?
- What instructional strategies do you use to teach literature?
- How can you integrate technology into your current strategies?

In this chapter we will explore online digital libraries and collections of online literature selections. You will find a listing of popular online libraries and other literary teaching resources in the Resources section of this text. Many of these texts are *hypertext* documents. Hypertext simply means that there are links within these documents that allow users to "link out" to various other sites for additional information. There are multiple differences in the reading process good readers employ when reading online text and reading printed text. Since we, as teachers of language arts, most likely believe in the value of the printed word, it is common to experience apprehension when dealing with online texts. This chapter presents the differences in reading online and reading printed texts so that you may see the advantages of each. After exploring the vastness of the cyberspace libraries, you will contribute to the learning community by discussing rationales for using cyberspace as a context for the study of and response to literature.

Communication technologies such as e-mail, instant messaging, and blogging are common to some of our adolescent students, but may not be part of our daily lives. These communication technologies offer new and different ways to explore and discuss responses to literature.

Northrop Frye, in his 1963 book, *Learning in Language and Literature*, has this to say about the teaching of literature:

> The ultimate purpose of teaching literature is not understanding, but the transferring of the imaginative habit of mind, the instinct to create a new form instead of idolizing an old one, from the laboratory of literature to the life of mankind. Society depends heavily for its well-being on the handful of people who are imaginative in this sense. (p. 58)

Realizing that Frye did not intend to speak to the changing of our society in reference to the changes technology would make, I cannot help but wonder about the relevance of the comment, "the instinct to create a new form instead of idolizing an old one." If you love teaching language arts partially because it is an opportunity to teach good literature, you may be a little uneasy about the effects technology has and will continue to have on the classic literature the majority of us read from printed pages. However, if you'll

consider for a moment the opportunity that comes from following
Frye's description of the instinct to create a new form instead of
idolizing an old one, you may see the vast opportunities that lie not
only in taking advantage of online literature, but also in allowing
students to extend their imaginations in responding to literature
through the wonders of technology.

In all literature classrooms there exists a fissure. It is most no-
table when language arts teachers attempt to answer the following
question: Will you assume the role of a knowledgeable interpreter
of the text's riches or that of a facilitator of student discovery?
This is the line that sometimes divides elementary language arts
teachers and high school English teachers. Is it best to be concerned with exploring the text in all of its historical, psychological,
biographical, and sociocultural richness, or should literature teachers be more concerned with exploring the students' responses to
literature and all of the historical, psychological, biographical, and
sociocultural richness found there?

There are multiple theories about the process humans use as
they read and comprehend any text. We will look at a three-phase
teaching cycle for the teaching of literature. The phases include
inquiring, connecting, and *engaging and elaborating.*

INQUIRING

During this component of reading, an understanding of the purpose of reading the literary model is critical to the student. Students enter the literature through this stage of reading. Teachers
must invite students to the literature during this stage. Technology
can enhance this stage through gateway activities such as building
background knowledge about the text, the author, or other readers' opinions of both. The development of graphic organizers or
diagrams can be useful during the inquiring phase. An example is a
tree diagram on which a student names a character from the work,

listing the qualities he or she admires about the character on the branches. Minilectures aided by technology presentations are also useful in front-loading instruction during this stage.

- Students often ask the teacher for clarification of the purpose for the literary model. Some requests for clarification are general, while others are very specific.
- Teachers or technology provide background information and invite the students to enter the story world.
- Students become engaged in the setting of the story.
- Students make predictions about characters and plot.
- Students set a reading goal that is primarily *aesthetic* (for pleasure) or *efferent* (for information).

In order to avoid using technology for technology's sake, it may be useful to consider the following questions before planning instruction:

1. How does your chosen technology activity activate or build on the students' prior knowledge or background information regarding your unit or theme?
2. How does technology work to motivate students for reading and inquiry regarding the theme or driving question of the lesson?
3. How will using technology help you organize the lesson inquiry, set goals, and consolidate learning about the theme throughout the unit?

CONNECTING

Remember to consider the purpose of the instructional content during this stage and avoid the danger of leading students toward a more knowledgeable teacher's foregone conclusions about the text. It is through this stage that students initially engage the text.

This category of reading includes the following processes:

1. Choosing a strategy for reading the text
2. Relating the current text to previously read texts, including not only printed text or hypertext but also media, music, art, and so forth
3. Identifying and relating to the social or cultural attitudes revealed by the characters or author
4. Showing or determining a degree of interest in the text or characters
5. Empathizing with the author or a character
6. Reflecting on memories or emotional experiences from the text or within the reader

It is in this stage that the students should realize that literature "belongs" to them, individually, rather than belonging to others, say, the writers of CliffsNotes or some literary scholar. In integrating technology into this stage of teaching, teachers should consider whether or not the technology and activities used require the reader to make literature come to life—to make it breathe, laugh and cry, or rejoice. Neither the technology nor the instruction should make the literature a thing to be regurgitated, analyzed, or categorized. Technology can enhance this stage of the process by providing students a medium through which to discuss good literature, providing avenues and means for speaking with authors or professionals in the field of writing and publishing, and helping students make literature personal through written and visual responses.

ENGAGING AND ELABORATING

Engaging and elaborating is the final stage of the three-stage method for teaching literature. During this stage, the readers' knowledge of text structures, their knowledge of literary elements and their functions, and the degree of interest in and purpose for reading fully develop. Characteristics of this category include

1. literal interpretation
2. symbolism
3. reflection on new knowledge
4. linking to additional information via hypertext links
5. relating to the author or the author's purpose
6. making further inferences about the literary model

If, through the course of our teaching by emphasizing each component of this three-phase cycle, students have inquired and entered the text, made connections, and come to care about the literature, then we can hope that they are ready to extend and explore new directions with the literature and interested in doing so. Technology can enhance this stage through responses to literature that involve the creation of projects involving multimedia presentation software, audiovisual presentations, or simply visual representations of literary responses.

"Why would I use online texts anyway?" you may ask. Consider this: So many quality pieces of literature are held in online libraries as online text. Having these texts available to your students at a moment's notice is invaluable. If you happen to be one of those classroom teachers who never has enough money for supplies or books, this may be part of the solution to your problem.

Knowing the differences in reading online hypertext and reading the traditional printed word is important when planning to implement online hypertext in your language arts courses. When students read literature from a printed text, they must read in a linear fashion. They often must stop to look up words, make connections among literary elements, or clarify their understanding. If they want to see information about the author of the text or critical reviews and comments on the literary text itself, they must locate and read yet another book. The student who would be forced to stop reading and pick up a dictionary or other text in order to make connections or build meaning from the original text no longer is forced to stop and search. Hypertext literary documents offer "clickable" links that provide information such as definitions, commentary, and author/genre information.

While students reading literary hypertexts may read differently, they do not necessarily respond to that literature differently. Technology opens up many avenues for literature response. It provides learners with multiple means of representing and acquiring new knowledge. It provides learners with multiple means of expression to allow them to demonstrate what they already know. It provides multiple means of engagement, allowing learners to express their personal interests and preferences for challenges, and to increase their motivation.

TECHNOLOGY FOR RESPONSE TO LITERATURE

When using technology to respond to literature, there are many options. Perhaps the most frequently used software for responding to literature is Microsoft's presentation software, PowerPoint. You will find many lesson plans that describe how students may use PowerPoint or other presentation software to create responses to literature. In the Resources section of this text you will find a sample of an eighth grade student's reading of and response to literature. Students can create presentations containing hypertext links within one PowerPoint document, or some basic Web page software can be used. Also within the Resources section for this chapter you will find a step-by-step guide for creating a PowerPoint presentation. You may wish to visit Education World's website, www.educationworld.com. Here you will find excellent Techtorials. PowerPoint allows students to find various media such as video, audio, visual, and text, to turn a response into a moving, living, perhaps yelling commentary on literature.

New methods of communication, such as e-mail, blogs, or discussion threads, also provide students with a venue for production of unique responses to literature. Since the common pattern of literature study in a classroom is teacher-led discussion which highlights and directs students' responses to specific "revealing" passages in literary text, these innovative communication technologies give new meaning to open, or guided, discussion. *Weblogs*, also called *blogs*, are Web pages created (in this case) by students and updated often. Students visit other students' pages and may respond to the interpretations of or responses to literature. Simple Web authoring software can be used to produce these pages, and there are a multitude of companies that provide free Web page hosting for students. Web authoring software will be discussed in later chapters. Web pages must be *hosted*, meaning that the *document* (Web page) must have space on a *server* (remote computer system) in order to be "posted" to the World Wide Web.

Students are probably most familiar with electronic mail as a means of communication. Students can set up accounts with companies that provide free e-mail. Most of your students are probably familiar with the services of Hotmail, Yahoo! America Online, and others. Educational topics such as responses to or interpretation of literature, that must be forced as discussion in classrooms, absolutely bloom online. When students are asked to e-mail one another about literary interpretations or responses and bring hard copies of that correspondence into class, motivation to discuss literature rises and critical thinking deepens. Implementing technology of this nature in your class requires that you set up the parameters for discussion and response. When given the opportunity to be creative in responding, some students will become "overachievers."

Some suggestions for possible projects that have students respond to literature using technology include the following:

- Have students write e-mails to each other as characters from a literary text.

- Build a website which explores relevant themes within novels and in texts beyond these novels.
- Juxtapose quotes from a literary text and music in a Power-Point presentation.
- Create digital collages of images that symbolize topics, mood, characters, and plot movement from a text.
- Ask students who participate in Facebook or MySpace to focus a section of their pages on academic work. (Doing so, and checking these sites, creates a community of adults who have the children's best interests at heart.)

Integrating technology into the teaching of literature takes time and patience. Remember that not everything you find on the World Wide Web is a reliable source of information. When students use literary hypertexts, they should be cautioned about the source of the document. This chapter has provided you with links to the most reliable resources on the Web. Continue to search, and build your collection of favorites in your searching. If you are reading this text as part of a learning community or study group, following through with the activities presented in this chapter will help you to address the International Society for Technology in Education's standards for teachers. Through incorporating technology as a means of reading, interpreting, and responding to literature, you are designing learning opportunities that apply technology-enhanced instructional strategies to support the diverse needs of learners.

As you select literary texts for students to access and read online, remember that the actual process of reading an online document may vary markedly from the process that same student would employ in reading a traditional text. Consider the complications and effectiveness of your reading strategies as you read this text. Provide time for students to adjust, but don't be too surprised if they already know how to adjust for the differences. After all, they are the "Nintendo generation," and they may have been blogging longer than you.

If you are reading this book as part of a learning community, you may want to complete the following activity: From the Resources section of this text, choose three online libraries to explore. Search for texts that you could use in class, but that you might not be able to obtain copies enough of to accommodate every student. As you explore, note the quality of the pages and follow a few hypertext links to see what additional information is provided. Turn to the Resources page for this chapter and choose three examples of student-generated responses to literature. Consider the use of multimedia to respond to the literature you teach in your own classroom. Consider the many uses of both hypertext literature and the communication technologies presented in this chapter. While reading online and reading print are very different, you can use the three-phase cycle to enhance both types of reading and responding to literature in your classroom. Be sure to discuss your thoughts with the members of your learning community.

REFERENCE

Frye, N., & MacKinnon, A. R. (1963). *Learning in language and literature: Insistent task in language and learning and the developing imagination.* Cambridge, MA: Harvard University Press.

4

SPINNING THE WEB
WITH CHILDREN'S AND
YOUNG ADULT LITERATURE

FOCUS QUESTIONS

- How do you currently use children's and young adult literature and the Internet to help motivate readers and foster a love of reading among students?
- Are you capitalizing on middle school readers' out-of-school literacies, as well as in-school literacies?
- How often do you explore online lesson plans and activities for using children's and young adult literature?
- Do you currently have a list of resources for use in teaching with children's and young adult literature, including both print and nonprint texts? Are you willing to organize your materials electronically?
- What strategies do you currently employ for using Inspiration, PowerPoint, or HyperStudio software for enhancing comprehension of young adult and children's literature?

The amount of teacher resources on the Internet is a little less abundant when language arts teachers move from classic literature to children's or young adult literature. However, there is still enough information jamming the information superhighway that teachers can become "stuck in traffic" for hours. No one, least of all a busy teacher, wants to waste endless hours searching for just the right lesson, activity, or background information, no matter how interesting the reading may be.

Finding useful information online becomes a little easier after you have mapped out a route—in other words, after you have carefully decided just what it is you're looking for and planned out a pathway for the search. We have discussed this topic in previous chapters. As you search the Internet, it is always a good idea to keep track of dependable sources and useful links. This can be done by creating a list of favorites in your Web browser. Use the following steps for finding and saving dependable and useful Web sites, in order to make your search for information more profitable and less time-consuming:

- Look for dependable websites:
    ○ Look for online professional organizations such as teachers' unions, professional associations, content area groups (International Reading Association [IRA] and National Council for Teachers of English [NCTE]), and technology groups. These sites commonly end in .org
    ○ Governmental sites are usually very comprehensive and have abundant resources for educators.
    ○ Education portals include information focused on education. Educational resources found at these portals may include teachers' guides to the Internet, online databases or journals, opportunities for student publication, or services such as free e-mail accounts, message boards, or website hosting.
- Plan 10 minutes daily, during the time you plan your lessons, to search for useful sites for use in both your planning and your students' activities.

- Build a favorites list for each class you teach. Keep information relevant only to that particular class's curriculum in each folder:
  - When searching in your Web browser (Explorer, Netscape, etc.), find and click the "favorites" tab in the top menu bar.
  - From the drop-down menu that appears, click "organize." A new dialog box appears.
  - In the dialog box, click "create a folder." A new folder is created, and you now have the option of naming the folder.
  - Some browsers require that you click "rename" in order to name the folder. It is a good idea to create a folder for each class you teach and a folder for general technology resources. This allows you to find information quickly without searching through a long list of various sites that you've found useful.
  - When you've found a new site you wish to add to your favorites, click the "favorites" tab on the top menu bar. Click "add to favorites." A list of your folders appears. Click the folder in which you wish the page to be saved. Click "ok."

If you're incorporating technology for the first time, it may be a good idea to let students know your goals for both your use and their use of technology. A team effort can help you build resources and motivate students to participate as members of your learning community. Create a bulletin board where students are allowed to post useful and dependable Web resources. You may want to require a checklist to help assure that the sites on the bulletin board meet your standards. This teaches students an important lesson about technology and the proper use of the Internet. It is a source of information, not knowledge! Both students and teachers must evaluate websites carefully.

Isn't the point of teaching this genre of literature to put a book in a child's hand and teach the child to love reading in an aesthetic manner, rather than teaching analytical or efferent reading? Well, that may be so, but research consistently indicates that teachers who implement technology in these areas of their language arts classes see wonderful benefits in student motivation, increased levels of critical thinking, and more and better student self-assessment (Colburn, 2001).

It is still important to put a book in a student's hand and teach him or her to "curl up with a good book," and that's a little difficult if the good book happens to be digital. So you're not ready to throw out the books and go online for every text you want your students to read. In chapter 3 we looked at the value of online text and discussed how the "Nintendo generation" is equally comfortable with hypertext or printed text. The benefits of technology in a language classroom go far beyond replacing printed words with hypertexts. It enhances all the activity that takes place in the three-step method for teaching/learning from books.

For example, when students are inquiring about a text, they ask teachers for direction in setting reading goals so that they can "enter the story world." Teachers may pose one question relative to the universal theme of a young adult novel, give pairs of students up to 15 minutes to search for information on the topic, and then have the student pairs join into groups of four in order to share information.

In Lois Lowry's book *The Giver*, Jonas, the main character, lives in a Utopian society. Students are usually shocked as they read and discover this fact. If not given some clues in a front-loaded lesson, students often become confused about the difficulties the characters experience in their perfect but limited world. The teacher who implements technology in order to assist students in building background knowledge can open up new and multiple definitions for "Utopia." Students then are allowed to synthesize this information so that it makes sense in the same context that Lowry uses it. They make connections to personal experiences and "enter the story world" more easily than students who are not offered this opportunity.

After students begin to understand the background information regarding a children's or young adult book, they then make connections by relating to the social and cultural attitudes revealed by the character or author. Technology also assists in this stage by helping students build stronger connections.

Sandra Cisneros's book *The House on Mango Street* is a series of vignettes. In one particular vignette, the main character, Esmeralda, discusses her name and its origins. It is sometimes difficult for children, or adults for that matter, to learn from or become comfortable with authors and characters from a culture other than their own. Teachers can help students make connections with this Latino culture by designing lessons that have students find information on Cisneros and other Latino authors. But it is important that students are not simply seeking information. The Internet is full of useless information, and students should be asked to process this information and use it to make connections with characters in the book. Teachers may design an online field trip to places that reveal information about this culture, its people, and their beliefs. Students can then write a description of the place they visited on their online field trip and share that information in the form of a travel brochure designed with software such as Microsoft's Publisher, thus finding information, synthesizing it, and sharing it with others through a creative activity.

Once students are intrigued by the information connected to their study of children's and young adult literature, they become more adept at the last phase of the three-phase cycle described in chapter 3. Intrinsic motivation takes up, and they begin to explore and extend on their own. If students do not reflect on this new knowledge, which is a characteristic of the engaging and elaborating phase, teachers can ask that students contribute to a classroom blog or online reading journal kept by the entire class. Students reflect on their own new knowledge and respond to the knowledge applications of their fellow readers. Children's books are often a great addition to longer novels when the goal is student engagement and elaboration on themes from longer young adult novels.

Derek Munson's children's book *Enemy Pie* teaches children not to judge one another too quickly. The person you thought was your enemy could just be your best friend. Although the book is relatively short, it is a children's book that works well as a read-aloud and can easily be related to classic poems or short stories. Students can explore the theme further by searching for recipes for "friendship pie" or the ingredients they believe friendship should include. Simple software programs can be used to create and publish "recipe cards" like the one in figure 4.1.

One often-overlooked goal of teaching with children's and young adult literature is that of making connections to classic literature. In chapter 3 you explored many sources for online hypertexts. The texts most often found in online libraries are those that are at least 20 years old. These books can be published in an online format much more easily than material with newer copyrights.

If you combine the information you've learned in these chapters, you should be able to make connections among children's and young adult literature and the classic literary canon. For example,

---

Friendship Pie

- 2 gallons of respect
- 5 tablespoons of smiles
- 1 cup of sharing
- 3 gallons of compliments
- 1 quart listening without interruption
- 2 cups of taking turns

Mix above ingredients together in 1 classroom. Add 1 teacher who contributes mutual respect, basic guidelines, and procedures to follow. Have all participants toss in 1 pound of fun every day. Bake at 80 degrees for one semester. Cut into 25 slices and consume a little each day.

Figure 4.1.   A sample "recipe" card.

Enemy Pie can be a follow-up or introductory lesson for more classic texts such as excerpts from Mark Twain's *The Adventures of
Huckleberry Finn*. Cisneros's *The House on Mango Street* comple-
ments Maya Angelou's *I Know Why the Caged Bird Sings*. While
parts of Angelou's book may be questionable for grades 6–8, chapter 16 can be used without concern. In this chapter, Margaret is
called Maya for the first time and contemplates the significance of
her name. Lois Lowry's classic young adult novel *The Giver*, with
its Utopian society, is a great companion for the traditional literary classic from George Orwell, *1984*, which presents a negative
Utopian or *dystopian* society.

Two forms of technology useful in creating responses to young
adult or children's literature are Inspiration and a simple presentation program such as Microsoft's PowerPoint. Both of these
software programs offer multiple opportunities and methods for
helping middle grades readers organize information as they read
and respond to the reading periodically while they read, rather
than after reading the text in its entirety.

USING INSPIRATION TO CREATE AN OUTLINE

The free version of Inspiration you may have downloaded and used
to generate the concept map in the learning community activity
in chapter 2 can also be used to create an outline. Follow these
simple directions:

Open your Inspiration software and immediately switch to the
"outline" view. To do this you will click on "outline" from the menu
bar. Type your main idea and then press Enter. Your cursor moves
below the main idea. This is an area where you can add notes about
the topic if needed.

Click the "add topics" button to add topics to your outline. Your
new topic is automatically inserted below your main idea and assigned a prefix.

To add subtopics simply move your pointer to the appropriate topic and click "add sub." A new subtopic is added. It is automatically indented and assigned a prefix. Once you have your outline design completed, you can move topics and subtopics by dragging and dropping. This is done by placing your pointer over the text to be moved, holding down the right mouse button and moving the text to its new position. Once you've reached the new placement for the text, drop it by releasing the right mouse button.

Save your work. You can change the view of your work by clicking on the "diagram" button in the menu bar. This allows you to see your outline in storyboard form rather than outline form. Any changes you make to your outline will be reflected in your storyboard, and vice versa.

USING INSPIRATION LANGUAGE ARTS TEMPLATES

Students can use features such as this to keep up with plot movement, character development or relationships, or settings. There are multiple templates for language arts that you may also find useful and easy to use.

From the "file" menu, select "template."

A dialog box will appear, showing your choices for template selection. Be sure to scroll down to see all of your options.

If you select the Language Arts—Vocabulary option, a template with nine empty ovals appears. One empty oval is highlighted. This is where you begin typing. There is no need to click anywhere. Just type the word you wish to be placed in this oval.

To type in one of the empty ovals, double click on it and type. Don't forget to click the text button at the bottom of the template and delete. The text listed there included instructions for using the template. As with any Inspiration document, you can toggle back and forth between the two basic views, "outline" and "concept map."

MOVING FROM INSPIRATION OUTLINES
TO MICROSOFT'S POWERPOINT
PRESENTATION SOFTWARE

The documents you or your students create in Inspiration can easily be transferred into PowerPoint for presentation to the entire class or groups of students. Having students create an outline as they read a young adult or children's book and then transferring that information to a presentation for the class can enhance comprehension and provide clarification for other, less adept readers. Follow these simple steps for converting Inspiration documents to PowerPoint:

Open one of the Inspiration documents you have created. Click on the "diagram" view. From the "file" menu, choose "export." A dialog box appears.

Choose "Microsoft PowerPoint RTF."

Open your PowerPoint software, either from a shortcut on your desktop or from your Start Menu. From the top toolbar in Power-Point, select "open existing presentation." You will need to change the "files of type" field to "all files." Inspiration exports all files as Word documents rather than presentations. Click the arrow to the right of the space where "all PowerPoint Presentations" appears. A drop-down menu appears. Click on "all files." Locate the document you exported from Inspiration, and click "ok."

Since Inspiration exports all documents as Word documents, you will need to use your PowerPoint skills to enhance the slide presentation. But the text is there!

ENHANCING A SLIDE IN POWERPOINT

You may choose to add a background to your slideshow. You can do this by clicking the "format" tab from the top menu bar. A new menu bar appears on the right side of your current PowerPoint presentation. Choose the slide format you like and click it. The format is applied to the entire slideshow.

You may choose to create your own original slideshows. If you do, you will need to select the "format" tab from the top menu bar. Then select "background." A dialog box appears. This offers the options for colors. Choose a color by clicking on the arrow for the drop-down menu in the background fill box. From here you are offered the option to apply the background to one slide or all slides.

You may also want to insert clip art into your slideshow. To do this, click on the "insert" tab on the top menu bar. Place your pointer over "picture" in the drop-down menu. You are offered the opportunity to insert a picture from your clip art collection or from other files, such as "My Pictures." Click either, find the picture you want to insert, and click the picture. It is automatically inserted onto the current slide. You can change the size of the picture or change its location by placing your pointer over the corners and dragging either one side or the entire picture.

Technology offers many creative options for responding to literature, be it literature of the classic literary canon or children's or young adult literature. It is beneficial for teachers of language arts to connect these two popular genres through technology. While children's and young adult literature is accessible to most middle school readers, once an aesthetic love of reading has been established and intrinsic motivation to read and respond to literature has been enhanced through the incorporation of technology, students are more likely to be motivated to tackle the more analytical aspects of classic literature and the analysis and interpretation of such.

It is advisable to stick with the books you are already accustomed to teaching. Choosing new reading material and planning to teach in a new way, or incorporate technology, will probably require too much time and cause an added amount of stress. Start with what you know and look for ways to enhance those texts. Begin looking for and organizing sites that offer not only background information and teaching ideas for you, but also activities for your students. These opportunities can include contributing to a learning community and communicating with others who have the same interests. Encourage students to assist you in finding these sites. Make a game of it. Collect the names and addresses of websites in a jar at the front of the room and visit one site each day. Reward the students who contribute to the jar. Involve your students in any way possible. This allows them to contribute and builds their self-esteem and motivation. Set technology goals for the entire class, yourself included, and have students monitor their goals while you monitor yours.

If you are reading this text as part of a study group or learning community, you may find it useful to complete the following assignments as a basis of discussion:

Use the Internet to search out lesson plans for a young adult novel or children's book you currently teach. You may choose to look at the samples in the Resources section for this chapter. After you've gleaned some creative ideas from the Internet, write a lesson plan using the following format.

1. Introduction: Introduce the topic of this lesson, the text, and the author. Teacher resources can be listed here.
2. Standards: List the IRA/NCTE standards and the International Society for Technology in Education National Educational Technology Standards addressed by this chapter. Links are provided in the Resources section for this chapter.
3. Overview of activities: Include a brief overview of the types of activities your students will be engaged in during the reading of the text.
4. Student resources, websites, and software needed to complete the activities
5. Assessment tools
6. Teacher prediction and reflection: If you haven't yet taught this lesson, make predictions about the successfulness of the

lesson. After you've had an opportunity to teach the lesson, reflect on the successes and the adjustments that may make the lesson stronger.

REFERENCE

Colburn, A. (2001). Changing faculty teaching techniques: A response to Flick and Bell. *Contemporary Issues in Technology and Teacher Education* (Online serial) *1*(1), 64–65. http://www.citejournal.org/vol1/iss1/frontpages/toc.html.

5

TECHNOLOGY, TALKING, AND LISTENING TO LEARN

FOCUS QUESTIONS

- What techniques have you used to encourage students to listen and talk as a strategy for learning?
- What methods for facilitating classroom discussion through the use of technology do you employ in your classroom?
- How do you assist students in adjusting their use of spoken and visual language to communicate effectively with a variety of audiences for a variety of purposes?
- How many lesson plans do you have that ask students to use audio technologies?

Teachers and educators often speak of the Language Arts. Can you name the six language arts? Having a thorough understanding of each of these six components of the language arts will enhance the way you think about and teach each of them. According to Tompkins (2005), teachers should design literacy experiences that include each of the six components of language arts—reading, writing, listening, speaking, viewing, and visually representing (see figure 5.1).

- *Reading*, or gaining meaning from print, is receptive written language. When we read, we interact with written language. We decode it, understand it, and take it in cognitively. Once a reader is fluent, this process occurs rapidly and effectively.
- *Writing* is the reciprocal of reading. When we write, we encode written language. Writing, then, is productive language.
- *Listening* is half of the oral language pair. When we listen, we receive and make sense of the oral language of others. Listening is receptive oral language.
- *Speaking* is the reciprocal of listening. Speaking, then, is productive oral language. Speaking and listening together are sometimes called *oracy*.
- *Viewing* is a receptive language arts skill. There is a fine line between gaining meaning from text that is heard and gaining meaning from text that is viewed.
- *Visually representing* parallels writing in that an individual produces something other than typical language, as in creating Web pages, movies, drawings, paintings, and other products of nonprint media. Like writing, visually representing is a productive skill.

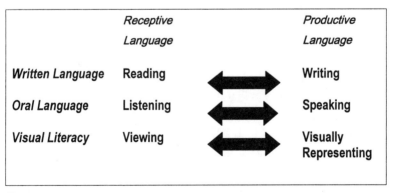

	Receptive Language		Productive Language
Written Language	Reading		**Writing**
Oral Language	Listening		**Speaking**
Visual Literacy	Viewing		**Visually Representing**

Figure 5.1. Relationships among the six language arts.

We will explore the oral language component of the six language arts. We will look at the relationship of talking, listening, thinking, and learning, and specifically how technology can enhance the learning that occurs through the oral language components of language arts. New communication technologies and simple audio clips can help students become better listeners and speakers. These features will open the doors of your classroom to a global learning community. There is much debate over the educational value of e-mail communication, discussion boards, interactive blogs, instant messaging programs, and communication tools provided by MySpace and Facebook. As teachers, we must be aware of the benefits and possibilities these new technologies hold for our students.

Audio and visual technologies have changed since the first half of the 20th century. The record players, tape players, and movie projectors of classrooms of the past have not completely gone away, but they have changed forms over the years. Rather than viewing movies by means of reel-to-reel projectors, teachers and students can now view streaming video over the Internet. Record players have evolved from large, round platters designed to play sound to cassette recorders, microcassette recorders, CD players, and MP3 players.

It is important to keep up with the fast pace at which technology changes the learning community, but it is equally important to remain focused on the importance of oral language in our classrooms. Every teacher uses an auditory delivery to present lessons to his or her students. Audio delivery is grounded in the learner's ability to listen attentively to the auditory stimulus. According to Barnes (1992), teachers claim that children who learn the value of talk as part of the learning process better understand and manipulate their own process of learning.

So how do we teach students to listen and speak so that they become skilled at both learning through their communication and learning from their communication? First we must understand the process of listening and speaking. If we plan to use audio or communication technologies successfully in our teaching, we must also teach our students to develop and practice the skills as a component of instruction.

Effective listening requires that the learner be able to hear accurately. Teachers should consider the environment in which the audio will be used. Often simple solutions such as additional speakers, curtains, area rugs, or cork wall materials can enhance audio presentations.

The second step in effective listening is focused listening. Have you ever found yourself listening to a lecture and drifting off to other thoughts? To listen to any auditory stimulus, you must give your full attention. Cognitive science tells us that it is normal for learners to shift this focused attention momentarily, but to return to the focus without much interruption. Schools do not often teach this critical component of listening. In order to improve your students' focused listening skills, you may want to play listening games. Check the Resources listing for this chapter for websites that offer listening games. If you have limited English proficient students in your classes, these games are excellent language development activities. They can provide any student with practice and assessment of his or her listening comprehension skills.

The third step in effective listening is reinforcement of the content. Think of the last time you listened to a lecture or a normal conversation about a new and complicated concept with which you were unfamiliar. Even if you listened carefully and focused on the points and details of the conversation or lecture, were you able to retain all of the information you heard? The answer is most likely no. For a new idea or concept to be integrated into your knowledge base, you need to reinforce it. Effective listening happens when attention is constantly refocused on the topic and when repetition restimulates neurons and builds new *dendrites*, or pathways to the information.

In order to be sure your students benefit from auditory presentation, you should take the following steps:

- Be sure that all students can hear the presentation.
- Ask students to focus their attention on the presentation, and provide multiple methods and opportunities for them to refocus. Keep their attention.
  - Explain the importance of listening closely.
  - Instruct children to look at the video, illustrations, or graphics that accompany the audio.
  - Watch for and teach nonverbal listening cues such as nodding your head or maintaining eye contact.
  - Have students restate the message or talk about the concept.
  - Allow students to ask questions, and encourage discussion.
- Provide reinforcement of the content through repetition and activities.

The second oral language skill is speaking, the reciprocal of listening. Did you notice that one way to assure that students are listening and refocusing is to allow them to communicate? Listening activities in classrooms should provide students the opportunity to participate in either whole-class or group discussions. When you plan for listening practice online, also plan a culminating activity that allows students the opportunity to speak.

There are online resources for this activity also. Students can record themselves speaking and upload these audio clips to your class Web pages. If your computer has a microphone and the proper software, you can create audio files. You will find many online tutorials for creating and maintaining a library of sound files. If you are a Mac user, you may enjoy "Creating Audio Podcasts on Mac OS X" at www.apple.com/quicktime/tutorials/podcasting.html. PC users may wish to see Educations World's Techtorial, "What is a Podcast?" and "Creating a Podcast" at www.educationworld.com/a_tech/archives/techtorials/html.

Audio and video have evolved so drastically in the past 50 years that it is difficult to keep up with the latest technological devices and their advancements. For example, do you own an MP3 player? How often do you use iTunes or download files to your handheld computer for listening? The sounds on the older audiotapes many of us listened to were stored in the traditional analog media. These were recorded using analog waves. Newer technologies store sound using *digitization*, or distinct bits, rather than analog waves. The result is a crisper, clear audio recording. There are many advantages to digital storage: higher capacity, greater durability, convenience in storage and handling, portability, and ease of use.

It is important that we teachers who wish to incorporate technology into our classes understand a little about Internet audio. We need to be aware of different formats and the hardware and software needed for its playback. The two most common formats of audio files found online are WAV files and MP3 files. WAV files are the digital version of analog audio. The sound or music clip has been converted directly into its digital counterpart. This is usually done through the computer's microphone. The audio is converted by the computer's sound card and software and then stored. WAV files maintain the quality of the original sound but are often very large files. In other words, WAV files take a considerable amount of space and time to download or upload. WAV files on the Internet are usually very short due to the size of the file.

A newer and faster audio format has been developed. *MP3* stands for Moving Picture Experts Group–1, Audio Layer 3. MP3 is an audio compression technology that gained popularity because is takes up much less space than WAV files. In order to play MP3 files you must have MP3 playback software installed on your computer. This is available for free download from the Internet. These files offer features that are especially useful for educational purposes. MP3 players support customized playlists as well as *visualizations*, or graphics and video clips. If you have RealPlayer, you're capable of listening to MP3s. There are sites that offer more detailed information on MP3s and "radio on demand" listed in the Resources section for this chapter.

USING MP3 AUDIO IN THE CLASSROOM

Perhaps the most obvious manner of using audio in your classroom is to add audio clips to your PowerPoint presentations or to teach your students how and why they should include audio in their presentations. There are simple steps for adding audio to Power-Points:

- Move to the slide where you want to insert the sound.
- Click "Insert" from the top menu bar.
- From the drop-down menu, click "Movie and Sound."
- Choose "Sound from a file."
- Browse for the file you have saved. Click the file.
- A speaker should appear in the slide. Click the speaker to test the sound.

A word of caution about jumping headlong into difficult audio technologies in your teaching practices is necessary here. While there are some simplistic uses of audio in your classrooms, most of the difficult work has been done for us by producers of easy-to-use audio software. It is advisable to integrate more simplistic uses of audio into your lessons to begin. Search for audio files that are useful in improving student listening, as well as those that enhance your own and your students' presentations. Plan time to read some of the suggested articles and additional links, and then prepare to practice with the more complicated audio and recording technologies.

Student and teacher presentations that employ sound are much more interesting and often more informative than presentations that only stimulate the visual sense. Incorporating sound into your PowerPoint presentations is simple.

First, you should search the Internet for audio files you can use, and save them to a file. Open the PowerPoint presentation in which you wish to insert an audio clip. If there is a particular slide in which you wish to insert the clip, go to that slide. From the top menu bar, click the "insert" menu tab. A drop-down menu appears.

From this menu, click on "movies and sounds." You may add sounds from your sound gallery or from the file in which you've saved the audio clips from the Internet.

Choose either option, as is appropriate to your needs. If you choose to insert sound from the sound gallery, you will be shown a new toolbar on the right side of your screen. This toolbar allows you to search for audio clips in the same manner that you search for clip art. In order to add the sound, simply double-click on the icon of your choice. You will be asked if you prefer the sound to start automatically when the slide displays, or if you would prefer the sound to begin when you click the mouse. A small speaker icon will appear on the slide, usually in the middle of the slide. You may click, drag, and drop this icon to the corner of the slide so that it is less distracting.

If you choose to insert a clip from your files, be sure to save your audio files to the "My Music" file, or create your own file called "audio clips."

We have looked at many uses of audio in the language arts classroom and discussed how central the skills of listening and speaking are to the development of both oral language and literacy. Advanced technologies are quickly changing, and the multimedia elements of audio and video change daily. It is essential for teachers to plan time to explore the options for implementing these advanced audio technologies in their lessons. However, it is advisable to implement these devices slowly, reading more about the uses of each one before it is implemented. Begin by searching the

Internet for lesson plans that include simple audio files. The Resources section of this text is filled with links to files that teachers or students may download and use in their presentations. These presentations can and should be used to generate class or group discussions. Activities such as these allow students to employ and hone both skills that make up oracy: listening and speaking.

By carefully choosing strategies for implementing audio in your language arts lessons, you will avoid overloading your preparation time and your tolerance for the new technologies. There is nothing more beneficial than technology used correctly and efficiently in a lesson, and nothing more frustrating than technology implemented before its use is fully understood and mastered.

If you are reading this text as part of a book study group or learning community, you may find it useful to complete the following activity and share your experiences with other members of the group. Begin with concepts and lessons you currently teach, and add audio gradually. If you're teaching literature, search for a clip of a poem, children's story, or fable that relates to the text you're teaching. You may also find clips from the author. Insert these clips into your presentation, or design a lesson that allows your students to search for clips that enhance their own presentations. Be sure to ask the students to clarify why the clip was useful. What purpose was there for inserting the sound? Did it have an emotional appeal? Did it refocus the listeners' attention on the presentation topic? Did it present new information?

REFERENCES

Barnes, D. (1992). *From communication to curriculum* (2nd ed.). Portsmouth, NH: Boynton/Cook.

Tompkins, G. (2005). *Language arts: Patterns of practice* (6th ed.). Upper Saddle River: Prentice Hall.

6

CYBER COMP: TECHNOLOGY TOOLS TO ENHANCE AND INSPIRE COMPOSITION

FOCUS QUESTIONS

- What strategies are you currently using to employ technology for inspiring writing and enabling writing?
- How do your students use technology to explore activities, and what are your instructional methods for assisting students to gather, synthesize, create, edit, and communicate knowledge through writing?
- What writing process do you use to teach composition? Do you believe that writing, like reading, varies by individual? Discuss the appropriate use of different writing process elements and the technologies that assist students in mastering each part of the process.

Exploring the many technologies that assist teachers in inspiring and enabling student authors can be beneficial to both teachers and students. We will take a look at the many methods and philosophies for teaching composition and relate each of these to the technologies that best enhance them. Throughout this chapter, you will be encouraged to visit multiple sites listed in the Resources section for this chapter. By exploring lesson plans and teacher resources online, you can continually build your list of favorites for future use in planning and in integrating technology into your language arts lessons.

Remember to look for places within your current classroom practices where you can incorporate technology, rather than beginning anew. It is helpful also to think of the previous chapters and the concepts learned in each. Remember that linking the language arts is very useful. You may find ways to enhance your units on children's stories and young adult literature or responses to reading assignments.

Writing pedagogy may be one of the most researched areas of middle grades language arts. Teachers, both experienced and novice, often feel that teaching the craft of writing is as mysterious as writing itself and far too complicated to be unguided. There are many viewpoints about teaching composition. Some believe a writing program in the middle grades should be very stiff and rigid, so that students learn the skills necessary to successfully complete state or national standardized tests. Others feel that the less structured method is better and allows for more student creativity and freedom. These are decisions you will make for yourself. As Graves (1975) once said, "We'll spend a lifetime crafting our teaching in order to allow children to be the authors of their own texts" (pp. 73–78).

No matter where you are on this spectrum of writing methodology, technology can enhance student writing. Many college composition classes are currently taught in computer labs, and students are required to compose and submit pieces of composition online—an environment this author has taught in many times. When looking out over the tops of monitors in a lab of this nature, it is easy to determine which students have been taught to take advantage of this new learning environment and which students have been taught in traditional pen-and-paper English classrooms.

Those students who were taught to take advantage of technology in writing usually compose as they type, and take the initiative to seek out sources for improving their writing available through software and online. Students who were taught in the more traditional methods feel the need to compose with pen and paper and then type their written work. They will often "stall out" when the need to use the software to edit or explore writing arises. There is room for balance. Research in higher education shows significant increases in the number of virtual writing workshops used to teach college composition courses. In order to better prepare our students for the global world of both college and the workforce, it is imperative that we offer them experiences with composition online.

As with all new tools of teaching, we should check our beliefs about teaching writing. Take a few minutes to think through this simple survey of assumptions about writing. Remember that each of us teaches our subject area differently, and finding the right combination of technology to fit our own personal teaching philosophy will assure success in implementing technology as a tool for teaching in each of our classrooms. Take a few moments to read through the following questions and decide how you feel about these aspects of teaching composition:

- Should teachers grade everything students write?
- Is grammar instruction in the middle grades most effectively embedded into writing instruction? Should it be taught directly?
- How much do students learn about the editing process when other students are allowed to edit their papers during peer editing sessions?
- Should students be asked to write about their own experiences and develop their own ideas about what they wish to write about?
- Which is more important in teaching writing, correctness and organization or clarity and substance of thought?

- Should grammatical conventions be emphasized only in the final edited version of a piece of student writing?

Strong (2006) suggests that there may be a hidden curriculum that surfaces with the instruction of composition. This hidden curriculum may include "school experiences that result in unintended, unplanned, even unsuspected and undesired student learning" (Shaver & Strong, 1982, p. 1). Incorporating the technology tools for teaching composition may increase the likelihood of a hidden curriculum. Strong advises us to unveil our own hidden curricula by considering the following statements:

- Writing in school is something you do to get a grade, and school is something you do to get a diploma or certificate.
- The main purpose of writing in school is to tell the teacher what the teacher already knows, not to explore a topic or idea.
- A second main purpose of school writing is to provide diversionary busy-work (or "time filler") so that the class is occupied.
- A third main purpose of school writing is to serve as a management threat to students or as actual punishment for misbehavior.
- The central intellectual activity in school writing is to guess what the teacher wants, not to figure out what's worth saying or how to say it most effectively.
- Information about required length is essential in school writing in order for you to pad appropriately or to minimize the possibility of doing extra work.
- Successful school writing takes no chances with ideas, thereby avoiding the risk of saying something interesting, important, or thought provoking.
- Good school writing uses a stilted, objective, and artificial voice—preferably heavy with ponderous words and vague abstractions.
- The best school writing uses a safe, conventional approach (short sentences, formulaic paragraphs, and mindless banalities) so that errors are minimized.

- Any type of personal writing (or writing on which one claims to have worked hard) automatically deserves a high grade, regardless of its features.
- Features of writing such as intelligence, quality of development, clarity and logical support are merely the subjective options of the teacher.
- Feedback from the teacher (responses, suggestions, and questions) are really corrections in disguise and their purpose is to justify the grade. (Strong, 2006, pp. 22–25)

As you learn more about technology tools that assist composition instruction, be aware of your beliefs and practices. Keep these in mind as you choose the most appropriate instructional tools and implement them in your classroom. Also, reflect often on the topics and lessons you employ to teach composition.

There are three commonly accepted approaches to writing: *process*, *product*, and *writing workshop*. All three have wonderfully supportive research foundations and practical applications in the classroom. You will find some works referenced in the Suggested Reading section for this chapter.

The process approach acknowledges the developmental work involved in any authentic and thoughtful writing, whether that of middle grades students or professional authors. If you use and are familiar with this approach, you may teach your students that even professional authors need extended amounts of time to prewrite, draft, and rewrite their works. For young writers, it often helps to draw clear lines between the parts of the writing process. Atwell (1998), Calkins (1994), Graves (1999), and Murray (2003) articulate a few basic assumptions upon which these approaches to writing rest. The list below explains how these basic assumptions can be connected to technology in composition instruction.

- *The writer is an autonomous self-starter who has a need to explore meaning and communicate.* All humans have an innate need to communicate, to tell their stories. Think of how often early adolescents talk to one another. Technology has offered this generation of adolescents new and more accessible methods for communication. How often have you heard a preteen pick up a cell phone to send a text message and suddenly stop typing because of writer's block? Our students are self-starters with an innate need to tell their stories, and technologies such as text messaging, instant messaging, and e-mail have made them more adept at communicating.

- *Writing is an extended process that includes prewriting, writing, and rewriting.* There are many different versions of "the writing process," and there are as many variations as there are writers. Each student, each writer may need a different process. It is good to teach that there are different steps, but to suggest that every writer must follow the exact same steps may obscure the process rather than clarifying it for individual writers. The forms of technology that encourage adolescents to communicate their stories more often may serve to keep students "chatting" through composition, and they may also have a negative impact on the writing that takes place in our classrooms. Students become so accustomed to using symbols rather than complete words that teachers must remind them often that the writing that is appropriate for text messages and e-mails is not always appropriate for every audience. The text generated in messages such as these can serve as a starting point for a form of prewriting, and can easily be moved through the entire process until it becomes a polished, almost translated piece of writing. Technology also offers many options for assisting students in reviewing and redrafting without having students literally rewrite every single word. Compositions generated through word processing software can be manipulated through multiple drafts, and students and teachers can use many tools to insert comments and track changes.

- *All modes of written discourse are equally respected.* Students may not realize how often they use writing in their daily lives. Atwell (1998), in her book *In the Middle*, suggests that teachers have students generate a list of "writing territories." This list may help students see the usefulness and necessity in writing. But do they see "school writing" as taking only one form? Technology can broaden how students think about writing. Word processors can be used to compose traditional student essays or projects, but there are so many more technology tools for enhancing writing, showing students that all modes of discourse are equally respected. This is easily accomplished by having students complete a scavenger hunt for various types of discourse on the Internet.

- *Students are expected to write and are given responsibility for shaping their own writing.* Responsibility does not come without choices. When students are given choices about what, where, and how to write, they make decisions that result in the teaching of self-disciplined writers. Offering opportunities for students to employ technology that motivates and makes writing more efficient helps to establish writing routines.

- *Conferencing with student writers is a basic feature of instruction.* The importance of face-to-face conversations with students cannot be argued. However, technology can make feedback from both peers and teachers immediate. If students are allowed to collaborate or peer edit their writing assignments, and they know that teachers accept and value these conversations that often take place through e-mail or instant messaging, students are more likely to discuss their writing routines, weaknesses, and strengths more often.

- *Student writers need many readers to respond to their work.* Technology has opened innumerable pathways for student publication, classroom Web pages, blogs, discussion boards provided by educational organizations, online poetry slams, etc.

- *Ownership of writing begins with selecting a topic and extends to giving writing a public platform.* Technology assists students from the beginning of the writing process through the end of the process. It can make the entire process more efficient and creative.
- *Writing is a whole process whose parts are not easily divisible but are recursive.*

The direct opposite of the process approach to writing is the product approach. Atwell (1998) contrasts these approaches in her book, *In the Middle.* As with any new approach to teaching, it is the classroom teacher who should reflect, measure, and determine which amounts of each approach make the best mixture for his or her own classroom. Table 6.1 lists some of the differences between these approaches.

Table 6.1. Two Approaches to Writing Instruction

Process Approach	Product Approach
1. Teachers assign topics.	1. Writing is self-initiated.
2. Most essays take the form of exposition. (A five-paragraph format is prominent.)	2. All modes of writing are equally respected, and students are encouraged to use each one at some point.
3. Direct instruction takes the form of daily language practice, mini-lessons, and student conferences. Grammar study and handbook rules are prominent.	3. Prewriting, writing, and rewriting lead to good writing.
4. Models and formal guidelines are used to assist students in producing good writing	4. The meaning of the writing piece determines the form of the writing piece.
5. Students are offered only one audience: the teacher.	5. Students' writings are made public to a variety of audiences.
6. Teacher-corrected papers are essential to the teaching effort.	6. Student–teacher and student–student conferences provide organization and assist students in writing like readers and reading like writers.

Writing workshops are common in middle grades language arts classrooms, and there isn't enough space within one chapter to provide a complete step-by-step guide for implementing writing workshops within your middle grades language arts classrooms. There are ample references and resources listed in this chapter to get you started on writing workshops. If you do not currently use this form of writing instruction, then read, research, and plan before implementing. Whether you are familiar with writing workshops or you're just interested enough to read through some of the information provided, you will be excited when you find out how easily technology is implemented in this form of teaching.

The basic principles of the writing workshop are communicated in table 6.1. In looking back at these principles, it is easy to see that a writing workshop is not simply a new physical arrangement for your writing class. The responsibility for writing and the actual work of writing shifts from the teacher to the students.

Technology is easily implemented in writing workshops through the three major components of the method:

Class time spent in full-tilt writing. A large amount of time spent in class on writing assignments allows teachers to groom increasingly independent authors. If you have the luxury of a writing lab, this time allows you to communicate individually with each author while others are continuously working on writing. Student work is more easily viewed in a word processor. Teachers can also more easily model their own writing process through the use of LCD projectors. This allows students to see and hear (if the teacher thinks aloud as he or she writes) the cognitive process writers use as they compose.

Ownership. Ownership is vital for middle grades students caught between childish dependence and more mature autonomy. Involving students in making decisions and experimenting with new technologies, and giving them independence in their writing, enables them to feel a sense of ownership. Teachers who allow students to form peer editing or writing groups with other students through electronic communication—perhaps within the same school, perhaps across the nation—allow their students to feel responsibility and ownership.

Response. Response is a vital ingredient to any composition classroom. Teachers who carefully create writing space in cyberspace allow students to have a library of reference material and writing models at their fingertips. They never have to leave their monitors to look up words, confer with others, or perhaps even ask the opinion of a real published author.

Each step of the writing process can be enhanced through technology integration. Prewriting activities are among the most abundant found on Internet lesson plan websites. Many different software applications can be used to enhance this stage of writing.

PREWRITING ACTIVITIES

Ghost Writing

For generating ideas, students may "ghost write" with a word processor. To do this, students simply turn the monitor off and type. It's like freewriting on a computer. No grammar checks, no spelling checks, no stopping places—just ideas flowing freely from the brain to the screen. When ideas are generated in a word processor they can easily be reorganized, prioritized, or evaluated so that the best topic is chosen from the writing.

Drawing

Most Microsoft software packages include a program called Paint. It can be found by going to the Start Menu, clicking on "all programs," clicking on "accessories," and then clicking on Paint. This program is easy to use and creates or edits drawings. Drawing often taps hidden thoughts and new connections for students. If the writing assignment involves a description of something, this program can serve as both an idea generator and an organizer.

Mapping and Outlining

We have seen in a previous chapter how Inspiration software can assist students in creating and annotating concept maps and outlines. This same software and the functions we have previously discussed can be applied to the creation and organization stages of writing.

DRAFTING

For successful writing, students must realize the importance of multiple drafts. While revising the first drafts of handwritten work requires students to rewrite every single word, documents created with a word processor offer students the opportunity to create and save first drafts for comparison or to create first drafts and then track changes to each draft until all changes have been made and the writing is polished.

REVISION

By *revision*, I do not mean implementing the changes suggested by the proofreading of peers or teachers. Revision begins with the author. It is important to teach students to revise their own work before sending it out for revision by others. This gives the author an opportunity to think through his or her rationale for writing in a certain way. These points, suggestions, or questions posed by the author can be inserted into the text of a document by inserting comments along the margins or by highlighting text. Second and third revisions by peers are often more productive when students edit and comment in writing through the "insert comment" function in their word processors. This gives the author and the reviewer a small amount of distance. For example, when we have students read their writing aloud to others in a group, the author is sometimes frightened of the feedback he or she will receive. The peer editors can also be afraid of hurting the author's feelings. Allowing students to suggest revisions on the document heightens the chances of having productive peer editing without management and discipline concerns.

PUBLISHING

Places that publish student writing are plentiful. Various national publications for young people solicit original writing. Making online publication opportunities available to students motivates student writers.

While many software programs are valuable in all stages of the writing process, none is as valuable as your word processor. Teachers can implement technology by simply allowing students to type their work into a Word document, print the document, and turn it in. But any teacher can achieve technology integration this way. The real issue with technology integration is not whether or not teachers use technology in their classrooms, but rather how well teachers integrate the technology into classroom instruction, so that students become actively involved in learning and the learning is enhanced by the technology. This goal takes a little more effort and motivation.

If students can open the word processor and type and save a document, they can also learn to make comments and track changes within their documents.

When you are ready to submit a document for editing or peer review, you may wish to first protect your document so that your original text remains intact. Use the following steps:

- Click on the "tools" tab from the top menu bar.
- Select "protect document." In newer versions of Word, a new menu bar appears on the right side of your screen. This menu offers you many options for protecting your document. You

may set format restrictions, editing restrictions, and groups who are allowed to edit.

- From this menu, select "editing restrictions." From the drop-down menu, select "tracked changes."
- Select "start enforcement." You will be asked to create a password in a dialog box.
- Create the password and click "ok."

You will also need to select the manner in which these changes appear in your document:

- From the top menu bar, select "tools."
- Select "options" from the drop-down menu.
- A new dialog box appears with multiple tabs.
- Select your choices and click "ok" to save your options. (Teachers may want to choose how all students' tracked changes appear.)

Those in each group (peer editors) will need to set the user information so that the author of the original document can determine which peer editor edited a particular part of the document:

- Select "tools" from the top menu bar.
- Select "options" from the drop-down menu.
- The same dialog box appears with multiple options. Select "user information."
- Type in your name and initials.
- Click "ok" to save your changes. As each person edits, his or her initials will be placed beside each comment.

Any text typed by a peer editor will now be marked to indicate a change, insertion, or deletion with respect to the author's original text. A black bar will appear in the margin to the left of any text that has been changed.

Adding a Comment

- Place your pointer over the point in the document at which you wish to comment.
- Click "insert" from the top tool bar.
- Click "comment" from the drop-down menu that appears. This will place a text bubble in the margin of the document. You may type your comment in this bubble. A line extends from the place in the document to the text bubble, showing the reader the association between the comment and that particular piece of text.
- When the peer editor has completed editing, he or she must save the changes to the document.

Authors can review and accept or reject changes. If the teacher wishes to see the work of the peer editors, the author can print the document so that the comments and suggestions are viewable.

Reviewing the Document

- Before accepting or rejecting any changes, authors will need to remove the document protection.
- Select "tools" from the top menu bar.
- Click on "unprotect document."
- Enter your password and click "ok."

You may now accept or reject changes:

- Select "view" from the top menu bar.
- Select "toolbar" from the drop-down menu.
- Select "reviewing" from this menu. You should now see three rows of "top" menu bars. The first is the bar with the labeled tabs: "file," "edit," "view," etc. The second consists of icons: a blank sheet of paper, an open file folder, etc.; and the third shows a drop-down menu option labeled "final showing

markup." There are eight icons that follow. If you place your pointer over each, the function appears in writing below your pointer. Find the icons that have the functions of rejecting and accepting changes.

- Click on the "accept change" button to accept the changes suggested by peer editors.
- Click the "reject change" button to reject the changes made by peer editors.

This chapter has presented many methods for implementing technology in the teaching of writing. Unlike in other chapters, we have not yet explored the multiple resources for implementation, the teacher resources, and the student resources. There are websites that offer lesson plans for using the Internet to inspire writing. Some of these plans are excellent and offer very creative opportunities for students and teachers to use the Internet for generating writing ideas and publishing writing ideas. Teachers who wish to implement technology in a manner that prepares their students to write effectively and efficiently in the workplace and in higher education courses should also consider giving students the writing skills they need to use a simple word processor to maximize all options.

Be sure to take a look at the resources recommended in this chapter for further information and lesson plan suggestions. Look critically at the lesson ideas you find online, and be sure that they assist students in using technology to communicate more effectively with others, as well as making learning fun through the use of technology.

When planning to implement technology in your own classrooms and lessons, begin with a lesson you currently teach so that you are not overwhelmed by the changes. If you do not currently employ a writing workshop approach, choose a composition lesson that you enjoy teaching and can easily enhance through the use of technology. True technology implementation in composition takes time and persistence. Generate a list of favorite sites and mark a folder for composition helpers.

In chapter 9 we will discuss the use of online writing labs (OWLs) and how these labs enhance student composition. There are links to some of those OWLs within the Resources section for this chapter also. These links offer wonderful ideas for teaching students to employ technology as they write. If you are reading this book as part of a book study group or a learning community, you may find it useful to complete the following activity and discuss the process and product with your group. This activity allows groups of students to use tables in a word processor to create a writing topology. Student groups swap topologies, which become the basis for a writing game that teaches the six elements of rhetoric. The extensions of this chapter have students complete a finished piece of writing using multiple formats. Study this activity, search the Internet, and create a lesson plan for implementing technology in one of your own composition lessons. When you've completed your lesson plan, share it with your colleagues.

REFERENCES

Atwell, N. (1998). *In the middle: New understandings about writing, reading and learning with adolescents* (2nd ed.). Upper Montclair, NJ: Boynton/Cook.

Calkins, L. (1994). *The art of teaching writing.* Portsmouth, NH: Heinemann.

Graves, D. (1999). *Bringing life into learning: Create a lasting literacy.* Portsmouth, NH: Heinemann.

Graves, D. (1975). The child, the writing process and the role of the professional. In W. Pety (Ed.), *The writing process of students* (pp. 73–78). Buffalo: State University of New York.

Murray, D. (2003). *A writer teaches writing* (2nd ed.). Boston, MA: Heinle.

Shaver, J. P., & Strong, W. (1982). *Facing value decisions: Rationale building for teachers* (2nd ed.). New York: Teachers College Press.

Strong, W. (2006). *Write or insight: Empowering content learning in grades 6–12.* Boston: Allyn & Bacon.

7

WORD WIZARDRY

- How often do you explore software for creation of word sorts, word games, semantic maps, etc.?
- What methods do you currently use for teaching vocabulary directly and indirectly?
- What types of board games or other vocabulary games or on-line word games, vocabulary lesson plans, or dictionaries do you currently use to teach vocabulary?

Research on the teaching of vocabulary clarifies that vocabulary instruction is an important part of comprehension instruction. Where does it fit into the process of comprehension? At all points. You'll recall that in chapters 3 and 4, when we looked at what happens during comprehension, we mentioned a three-phase cycle that included inquiring, making connections, and engaging and elaborating. Well, vocabulary instruction should take place during each of these stages of the comprehension process. In other words, your students need strategies for exploring new vocabulary during prereading activities. These are often teacher selected and guided by the teacher. Students also need to know, and need to be able to use, strategies for building meaning from words during reading. There are many methods for teaching these skills. Before we go deeper into the topic of teaching vocabulary, it's probably a good idea for you to take a few minutes to think about how you teach vocabulary.

I was a product of *direct vocabulary instruction* during middle school and high school. My teachers would find a good vocabulary workbook, introduce the new chapters on Mondays, provide a little practice during the week, and give vocabulary tests on Fridays. Did it work? Yes and no. Let's see . . . during my senior year of high school, I attended school for 36 weeks. I learned 20 new vocabulary words each week. I know this because I always made 100 on my vocabulary tests. That means that during my senior year of high school, I acquired 720 new vocabulary words! Why is it, then, that the only one I can recall is *cacophony*?

During my years in graduate school, I began to question my own teaching practices. I focused on vocabulary instruction when I first read Allen's (1999) book *Words, Words, Words: Teaching Vocabulary in Grades 4–12*. I began to wonder what the connection was between definitional information and comprehension. Researchers Baumann and Kameenui (1991) found that looking up definitions and synonyms did not improve students' understanding of vocabulary words. If you take a look at almost any middle grades reading text, you'll see that the vocabulary words students must know in order to comprehend the text are almost always listed. Many of the newer texts list only a few words before the story and follow those with additional words, either highlighted or in bold print, within the story.

If you are teaching a novel and using a novel guide to guide your instruction, there may be lists of vocabulary words included. The importance of learning the new vocabulary necessary for comprehending the main ideas of the text cannot be overstated. Your beliefs about how many words to teach and which words to teach will impact the methods you choose for vocabulary instruction. Through experimentation with self-selected vocabulary, word games and puzzles, speaking exercises, and various vocabulary assessments, I determined that the best vocabulary instruction for my students was a combination of direct and indirect vocabulary instruction throughout the teaching of any text—be it online or in print, short story, poem, or grammar text. To this day, I still believe that it takes more than definitional information regarding a word to actually *know* a word.

Ultimately, I determined that it was most important that I teach students how to build their own vocabulary and instill in them an understanding of the importance of learning new words. Whenever I wanted to know if my students truly *knew* a word, I would not just ask them to match the word to its correct definition. I'd ask them to use the words in speaking, in writing, and in wordplay. I developed a quick guide for building vocabulary from my own reading experiences and research on the topic. This guide was displayed on my classroom wall and often became a springboard for discussion after missed opportunities to truly learn a new word. See table 7.1 for a sample of this guide.

The fluent readers in my classroom already knew some of these skills for building their vocabulary. They had learned these during reading instruction, not through looking up definitions of preselected vocabulary words. The guide I developed for building vocabulary assisted my struggling readers, perhaps more than any direct vocabulary teaching I had ever done. Does this mean that direct vocabulary instruction is ineffective? No, but direct vocabulary instruction is most effective in the following contexts:

- Only a few words central to the content of the story or informational text are taught.
- Words are taught in meaningful contexts that convey the particular meanings relevant to the text.

Table 7.1. Building Your Vocabulary Every Day

Learn roots, prefixes, and suffixes.	Keep a list of these and their meanings. They will help you in *inferring* the meanings of unfamiliar words.	Apply this knowledge as you encounter words in your reading at home and at school.
Use context clues.	Take a look at the words around an unfamiliar word. Learn the different types of context clues.	Context clues can include definitions, synonyms, comparisons, contrasts, restatements, items in a series, tone, and cause and effect.
Use your dictionary, your thesaurus, and a vocabulary journal.	Look up words you do not know if you can't determine the meaning through inference or context clues. List the word in your vocabulary journal and write a definition *in your own words.*	

- The teaching of vocabulary is integrated with the activation and development of prior knowledge.
- Teachers teach words thoroughly by offering students rich and varied information about them.
- Students are exposed to one word many times.
- Students are actively involved in the process of learning the words.
- Words are taught before, during, and after reading.

Allen (1999) suggests that vocabulary development be supported in a variety of ways. Her suggested methods apply to both direct and indirect vocabulary instruction:

- Repeat words in varied contexts.
- Describe words.
- Support words with visuals.

- Connect words to students' lives.
- Extend words with anecdotes.
- Make associations.
- Compare and contrast words.
- Question words.
- Rephrase sentences and definitions.
- Provide tactile examples.

Think of the last vocabulary lesson you taught. Did you use any of these methods? Many textbook companies offer ancillary materials to help you teach vocabulary. Sometimes these are useful, but at other times teachers feel they need to create their own vocabulary teaching tools. Look carefully at Allen's list and decide what activities you use in your own classroom to support student vocabulary development. Do you use chart paper to draw KWL charts? Knowledge ratings? Semantic feature analysis grids? Perhaps you draw these out and run copies for individual students? There are many ways in which simple software programs can assist you in developing teaching materials. It's important to remember that the goal of all vocabulary development is to help students become independent learners who have strategies for inferring the meanings of unknown words when they encounter them.

In this chapter, we're going to focus more on how to integrate technology into your vocabulary instruction. Whenever you use technology to support vocabulary instruction, it should lead to independence in vocabulary learning, in the same way that instruction without technology would lead to independence in vocabulary learning. The decision about whether or not to use technology as part of vocabulary instruction should always be based on whether or not the tools will improve student learning outcomes. As you seek to infuse vocabulary instruction with technology, keep these goals in mind:

- Technology should help students relate new vocabulary to their background knowledge.

- Technology instruction should help students develop extensive word knowledge.
- Technology instruction should provide for active student involvement in new vocabulary.
- Technology instruction should develop students' strategies for acquiring new vocabulary independence.

You can develop vocabulary teaching materials by downloading online *freeware*. Freeware simply means software that is free for download onto your computer for your use and your students' use. The freeware programs available can help you generate crossword puzzles, word searches, hangman games, and many other word games. Wordplay is important in providing rehearsal of words, spellings, and meanings so that students remember the words. They'll then be more likely to use these new vocabulary words in their speaking and writing. Many useful sites for vocabulary freeware are listed in the Resources section of this text. Take some time to play with the games and generate some puzzles. Who knows—maybe you'll even build your own vocabulary while playing with the tools!

Simple software programs can also be used to create vocabulary materials. Your word processor will allow you to build many useful charts using the "table" feature. For example, a *knowledge rating* like the one shown in table 7.2 can be developed by inserting a simple table into a Word document.

Tables in Word documents are useful for many other vocabulary materials. *Semantic feature analysis grids* allow students to examine related concepts but make distinctions between them according

Table 7.2. A Knowledge Rating

	Know It.	Heard of It.	No clue!
1. bibliophile			
2. atypical			
3. macrocosm			

to particular criteria across which the concepts can be compared. These grids can be created by teachers for students, or students can create their own grids to share among student groups. Concept maps are a very effective strategy for teaching vocabulary. Students can use Inspiration software, or concept maps can be created using a simple word processor. Concept maps in various forms are useful for vocabulary instruction. The main reason for using such maps to learn words is that it's not enough to know the definition of a word. Students know a word better if they can create a visual (the map) that allows them to describe the characteristics and elements of the word and its relationship to other words or concepts. The concept map shown in figure 7.1 is one example of the various concept maps used for vocabulary instruction. Before you have students create their own concept maps for vocabulary words, think about the connections, relationships, examples, nonexamples, and elements you want students to see. You may add different parts to the map and organize them differently. Students can also determine how to build their own concept maps for words. Allen (1999) offers many examples.

Another excellent way to integrate technology into vocabulary instruction is to send students on a virtual word scavenger hunt on the Internet. Scavenger hunts help students build meaning by collecting virtual items and pictures, and they are valuable because they are fun, they develop cooperative learning skills, and they require active involvement. This is usually done in small groups. The teacher can preselect vocabulary words. This list of words

Table 7.3. Understanding Characters through Traits

	Gossipy	Quarrelsome	Eccentric	Domineering	Quixotic	Steadfast
Marilla						
Matthew						
Diana Barry						
Gilbert Blythe						
Ms. Rachel Lynde						
Miss Muriel Stacy						

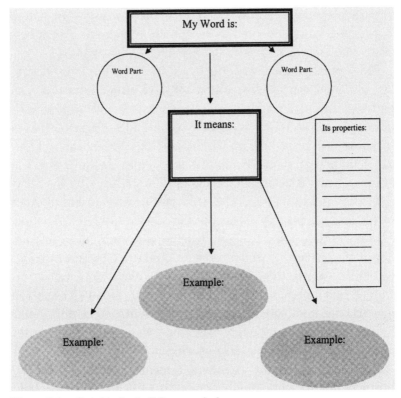

Figure 7.1. A guide for building vocabulary.

should use three types of vocabulary words: general, specialized, and technical.

In order to create an Internet scavenger hunt, you'll need to first prepare a master list of vocabulary words and distribute it among students. You'll then need to ask them to go out and find examples of these words being used (in any type of medium). Team members can be assigned specific roles, to keep the group focused and active. Roles may include a "path tracker" who keeps track of each site visited by the group, an "artistic designer" who plans and communicates the visual elements of the culminating activity, a "master searcher" who leads the search, and a "time manager" who keeps the group on track and aware of time constraints. This activity can take one class period or up to one week. Teachers can offer some options for culminating activities and products. Some examples include collages with words and pictures (made with word processors), slideshows of illustrations, and graphic organizers like those found in Allen's (1999) book *Words, Word, Words*. Audio clips can be generated (with presentation software), picture books can be designed through slideshows, newspapers or comic strips can be generated using Microsoft Publisher, and finally an exhibit can be held for students to display and explain their work.

If you have students in your room who are visual learners, you might want to ask them to do a different sort of vocabulary project. Vocabulary cartoons can be a very effective way for visual learners to demonstrate their understanding of new words. These activities have students create *mnemonic devices* and illustrate them. Mnemonics arc devices which help organize information so that students remember that information more easily. There are many kinds of mnemonic devices. Please see table 7.4 for examples.

The mnemonic device best suited for helping students build vocabulary is the key word method found in table 7.4. To use this method, begin with a target word.

The target word should be associated with a *concrete word(s)* that is familiar to the student. This concrete word becomes the key word and should be acoustically similar to the target word. Students then relate the concrete key word to the target word in an interactive picture. For example, the target word *passive* can be related to a key word, *massive*. *Massive* is a concrete word that is easy to visualize and acoustically similar to the target word. Students now must relate these two words in an interactive picture. They may create a sentence using both words and then insert an image or a set of pictures that shows the relationship: *Fat Cat was so massive that she had no choice but to be passive.* Students would then draw a picture of an inactive, massive cat.

Table 7.4. Mnemonic Devices

Acronym—an invented combination of letters, with each letter acting as a cue to an idea you need to remember.

BRASS is an acronym for how to shoot a rifle: Breathe, Relax, Aim, Sight, Squeeze.

Acrostic—an invented sentence where the first letter of each word is a cue to an idea you need to remember.

EVERY GOOD BOY DESERVES FUN is an acrostic to remember the order of the G-clef notes on sheet music: E, G, B, D, F.

Rhyme Keys—a 2-step memory process:
1. Memorize key words that can be associated with numbers (one–bun).
2. Create images of the items you need to remember, using the key words. (A bun with cheese on it will remind me of dairy products.)

To remember **food groups**:
1. Dairy products: one–bun–cheese on a bun.
2. Meat, fish, and poultry: two–shoe–livestock with shoes.
3. Grains: three–tree–sack of grain hanging from a tree.
4. Fruits and vegetables: four–door–opening a door and walking into a room stocked with fruits and vegetables.

Loci Method—a technique whereby you imagine placing the items you want to remember in specific locations in a room with which you are familiar.

To remember **presidents**:
Place a dollar bill (Washington) on the door. Walk into the room and see Jefferson reclining on a sofa and Nixon eating out of the refrigerator.

Key Word Method—a technique whereby you select the foreign words you need to remember and then identify an English word that sounds like each foreign one. You then visualize an image that involves the key word with the English meaning of the foreign word.

In Spanish, the word *cabina* means "phone booth." Visualize a cab trying to fit into a phone booth. When you see the word *cabina*, you should be able to recall this image and thereby retrieve the meaning "phone booth."

Figure–Name Technique—a method whereby you invent a relationship between the name and the physical characteristics of the person.

To remember the name **Shirley Temple**: Visualize her curly (rhymes with "Shirley") hair around her temples.

Chaining—a technique whereby you create a story in which each word or idea you have to remember will cue the next idea you need to recall.

To remember the items **Napoleon, ear, door,** and **Germany**: Create this story: **Napoleon** had his **ear** to the **door** to listen to the **Germans** in his beer cellar.

Vocabulary activities can be enhanced with technology. Let's examine, more specifically, some of the technology tools previously mentioned, such as creating tables in Word, using the AutoShapes feature to create a concept map if you don't have access to Inspiration software, and, finally, using the Paint program to help your students create freehand art to demonstrate their understanding. If you are completing the suggested activities at the end of each chapter, you have created tables in a Word document. Since you already know how to create a table, let's focus on the ways that you can modify and enhance tables with some very simple adjustments.

MODIFYING TABLES

Once you or your students have inserted a table into a document, you can change the appearance of the table by highlighting your table and clicking on "table" from the top menu bar. From the drop-down menu, click on "autoformat" to see the options for automatically formatted tables.

If you've inserted table headings into your table and discover that your headings are too long to be displayed horizontally into a table cell, you can adjust the headings so that they appear vertically instead. Simply highlight the row containing your headings and click on "format" from the top menu bar. From the drop-down menu, click "text direction" and choose the format showing the text direction you want to use.

USING AUTOSHAPES

If you don't have a concept map program such as Inspiration, you and your students can create concept maps using the AutoShapes feature in your Microsoft word processor, spreadsheet program, or presentation software. This feature is found on the lower toolbar on your screen and, right next to the word "AutoShapes," you'll see a drop-down menu indicator.

If you click on this indicator, you can see your options for AutoShapes. There are many options for callouts, arrows, charts, etc. Also along this toolbar you'll find a simple line, an arrow, a rectangle, an oval, and a diagram or organization chart. These options from this lower toolbar allow you to automatically insert these images into your document. Once inserted, each image can be altered to meet your needs. Below are the steps for modifying an AutoShape.

To make changes to an AutoShape, click on the shape in your document that you wish to change.

- To move it, simply drag it to the desired location.
- To change the size, click on the corners, sides, or upper or lower lines and draw them until the object is resized.
- To change the color inside the shape, click on the "fill" button on the "draw" toolbar at the bottom of the screen. Click on one of the colors in the current color scheme, or click on "more colors" to see more color options.
- To change the shape's outline colors, click on the "outline" button on the "draw" toolbar.
- To add shadows or give 3-D looks to the image, click on the "shadow" button or the "3-D" button on the "draw" toolbar.
- You can group shapes together and work with them as though they were one object by pressing the shift key and clicking on the AutoShapes. Then click the "draw" button on the "draw" toolbar and select "group."

All Microsoft Office programs come with a standard Paint program. To find this program on your computer, go to "start," then go to "accessories," and then go to Paint. This program allows students to create artwork freehand and then manipulate those images using the functions in the left-hand palette. This program also allows students to work with images such as digital pictures that may have been scanned into the computer. All Paint images can be placed into any other Microsoft program, such as PowerPoint, Excel, Word, and so forth, by simply cutting and pasting. Follow this link for a brief, but very informative, explanation of how to use Paint:

www.lkwdpl.org/classes/MSPaint/paint.html.

As with any other new method for teaching, new vocabulary methods work best when you first reflect on your beliefs about vocabulary instruction. Reflection is, after all, a very important part of teaching! The next step is to think about ways to incorporate technology into your vocabulary, in ways that enhance your students' understanding.

Once you've tried a few of the suggestions for implementing technology in your vocabulary lesson, reflect on your students' success and comfort with the method and the technology, as well as your own feelings about the lesson. Continue to adjust and manipulate the lessons until they bring about more positive learning outcomes for your students.

Remember that in implementing technology in vocabulary instruction, the following should be evident:

- Technology should help students relate new vocabulary to their background knowledge.
- Technology instruction should help students develop extensive word knowledge.
- Technology instruction should provide for active student involvement in new vocabulary.
- Technology instruction should develop students' strategies for acquiring new vocabulary independence.

When planning new vocabulary lessons that integrate technology, it may be easier to begin with a lesson you've already used. For example, do you currently have your students use traditional art media such as crayons, markers, or paint for drawing vocabulary cartoons? If so, this may be a good place to begin implementing the technology of Microsoft's Paint. You're already familiar with the context of the lesson, and you know what needs to be adjusted to improve the lesson. You're more likely to be satisfied and successful by beginning here in your comfort zone and stepping out a little at a time, and you are less likely to give up too easily.

If you are reading this book as an active member of a learning community or as a book study participant, you may find it useful to complete the following activity and share those experiences with your colleagues:

After viewing some of the suggested websites in this chapter, create a lesson plan for use in your classroom, where students use some of the technology that was described in this chapter to acquire a better understanding of vocabulary words.

You may use the template found in the Resources section. In your lesson plan, be sure to list the standards for English language arts and the technology standards that are addressed in your lesson. When you've completed your lesson plan, share it with colleagues. Explain what challenges, if any, you had in developing the lesson, and discuss challenges or opportunities you foresee in implementing the lesson. If you've had the opportunity to teach the lesson, collect and analyze student work samples.

REFERENCES

Allen, J. (1999). *Words, words, words: Teaching vocabulary in grades 4–12.* York, ME: Stenhouse.

Baumann, J. F., & Kameenui, E. J. (1991). Research on vocabulary instruction: Ode to Voltaire. In J. Flood, J. M. Jensen, D. Lapp, & J. R. Squire (Eds.), *Handbook on teaching the English language arts* (pp. 604–632). New York: Macmillan.

8

VISUALIZING VERSE ONLINE

FOCUS QUESTIONS

- In your personal reading of poetry, how often do you respond in writing?
- What websites do you currently use for your personal purposes to read, analyze, or enjoy verse? Do your instructional practices include references to these sites?
- How and how often do you include Internet resources for reading or responding to poetry?
- Describe the best lesson you've ever taught involving technology and poetry. What level of technological knowledge and ability did this lesson require of your students? What was their response to the technology?

In this chapter, we'll explore the creative and technical side of poetry. Reflecting on your experiences and feelings about writing poetry, reading and responding to poetry, and analyzing poems will assist you in this endeavor. It's important, here again, to reflect on our personal teaching styles where teaching poetry is concerned, as well as our objectives and goals for teaching poetry. In this chapter we will look at the purposes of poetry in language arts instruction.

Before we begin infusing technology tools into your instruction of poetry units, you should consider your preferences and beliefs about how, when, and why you include poetry instruction in your language arts classrooms.

How would you describe your personal response to poetry? Do you approach poems with devotion and savor every symbol, metaphor, and literary device? Maybe you're only mildly interested in poems and typically prefer some other genre of literature. If you've had bad experiences with writing or reading poetry, you may be apprehensive about having your students write poems or study poetry. Reflect for a few minutes here on the major factors influencing your feelings about poetry.

There are many ways to teach poetry, and the method your language arts teacher used to teach poetry when you were in school or college may impact how you teach the genre to your own students. Think through the following list, determine how you were taught, and see if your instruction parallels the way you were taught:

- Oral reading of poems
- Historical context of poems and poets
- Authorial biography
- Analysis of form
- Discussion of ideas
- Connections with personal experience
- Performances

Students know, without being told, their teachers' preferences for particular genres, authors, technology tools, or topics in language arts. What preferences do you think you're communicating to your students when you teach poetry? What impact will this have on their learning outcomes? These are important questions to ponder.

In my own teaching experience from sixth grade to college, poetry seemed to be the genre that my students either really loved or
hated. There wasn't much middle ground. Does any of this sound
familiar? Technology can be the hook that motivates some adolescents to read and even write their own poetry. As you read through
this chapter and begin to implement technology tools in your
teaching of poetry, remember to monitor your goal for the implementation. Is it technology for technology's sake, or will it truly
enhance your students' understanding of and love for poetry?

FOUND POEMS

Found poetry is poetry created by taking portions of any form of
text where words simply have the sound of poetry. Students search
out unintentional utterances of poetic language in advertisements,
instructions, expositions, etc. Perhaps you have used this technique
for writing poems without the use of technology. This is one of the
simplest places to incorporate technology into poetry. Poetry can
be found in innumerable places if students are taught how to look.
These poems begin as inadvertent utterances of poetry in typically
nonpoetic contexts, including newspapers, advertisements, conversations, and product instructions. When technology is added
as a tool for teaching found poetry, students can find these unintentional utterances in lots of unexpected places, such as pop-ups,
online advertisements, educational websites, commercial websites,
product descriptions . . . and even in threaded online discussions.
    Try sending your students on a guided or unguided treasure
hunt on the Internet. Students should be directed to look through
multiple websites in search of unintentional poetical utterances.
This also assists students in recognizing onomatopoeia, alliteration,
consonance, and other poetical devices. If you allow your students
to use audio as well as text, this search and discovery mission can
yield lessons in listening, talking, reading, writing, classifying, and

clarifying skills. The purposes of found poetry assignments should include:

- an awakening of students to the poetry used every day
- student exposure to unexpected realities and the significance of everyday happenings
- the startling impact words and images can have on readers
- a movement of students to more classic poems

Using technology to teach found poetry provides students with experience and skill in searching the Internet, as well as in using a browser. When students have found pieces of poems they wish to include in their found poems, they learn to rearrange syntax, compress phrases, and repeat key words. These tasks are simplified even further if you ask your students to use a word processor to write and edit the poems. Table 8.1 describes some guidelines for finding and writing found poems.

MUSIC

Music is always an appealing way to get students hooked on poetry. The use of music to teach poetry, like found poems, reinforces the fact that poetry is not out of the ordinary sphere of human experience. And I'm sure your middle school students would love any activity that involves music! After all, it's often at the center of their lives. The most difficult aspect of teaching poetry through music is often finding the right music and then locating the lyrics to the songs. This is where the Internet can be really helpful—lyrics are abundant on the Internet.

Teachers who wish to have students locate lyrics and then draw connections between lyrics and poetry may need to teach some common elements such as rhyme, meter, images, figures, symbols, and refrains. Students can use tables in Word documents to create

Table 8.1. Guidelines for Finding and Writing Found Poems

Search the Internet for online journal articles, textbooks, instruction manuals, directions, instructions, advertisements, personal ads, want ads—any nonliterary source—for hidden poetic phrases.

Cut and paste at least three phrases into a Word document, where you place what you consider the most interesting words at the ends of the lines to give them the greatest emphasis.

Do not add words or change the original material.

You may add a title and space and break the words any way you wish to create new meanings or sound effects. Search for hidden ironies, puns, and incongruities. The result may be serious, shocking, ironic, sarcastic, clever, or humorous.

Repeat key words or gather words to create a refrain.

Use white space carefully and illustrate if needed.

graphic organizers to show likenesses and differences in poems and lyrics. You'll recall we talked about how to create tables in Word in previous chapters.

Music can also be used as an accompaniment to poetry. Students can be taught to make connections between words and music that animate each other. Teachers may want to emphasize the fact that many early English ballads began as songs rather than poems. Many modern composers have written music to accompany poems, and their audio clips can be found online and incorporated into PowerPoint presentations as accompaniment to student-written poems or classic poetry. Can you imagine how jazzed up your students would be if they could play music to complement and enhance their poetry?

PATTERNED POEMS

Many teachers find patterned poems useful in teaching other concepts in language arts. These poems follow a specific format or template. They are effective with young writers and reluctant poets because they provide a structure that doesn't require the writer to thoroughly understand the intricate form of poetry. Students can be engaged in careful word choice without the intimidation of the usual elements of poetry, such as meter and rhyme. Patterned poems such as biopoems, diamantes, and acrostics are opportunities for you to create a template in your word processor which your students can then use when they write patterned poems using their word processors. What's really great about the template is that you can use it over and over again! Creating a template is as easy as 1-2-3. First, you type the requirements for the patterned poem, then save the document as a template. Finally, you instruct your students to open the template before writing their poems. Here's a step-by-step guideline for creating templates in Word:

- Open a new document in Word.
- Create/type the document that describes the pattern.
- Save the document.
- In the "save" dialog box that appears, find the "save as type" line near the bottom and click the drop-down menu.
- Choose "document template" from the drop-down menu.

When you want your students to use this template to create a poem, have them open a new document and select your template from the template menu that appears on the right side of the screen. If your students work in a lab, you'll have to post this template option on the network so that all students can access it when needed.

Templates can also be created for fixed forms of poems such as sonnets, limericks, haikus, chinquapins, and diamantes.

CONCRETE POEMS

The creative elements of a concrete poem allow teachers to implement technology tools such as those described in the previous chapter of this text. Students can use the Paint program to design artwork, and they type the text of the poem into or over the art. Students can also fill AutoShapes in with poems, or they may simply play with fonts, colors, and white space in a Word document.

POETRY NOTEBOOKS, SCRAPBOOKS, AND PORTFOLIOS

Many teachers require students to complete an entire unit on poetry and then assign the creation of a poetry notebook as a culminating activity. These notebooks have varied components, stem from diverse goals, and can take an assortment of shapes. Some teachers may call them *poetry scrapbooks* and still fewer refer to them as *poetry portfolios*. There is one distinct difference between a notebook or scrapbook and a true portfolio.

Poetry portfolios require statements of reflection about the artifacts included in the portfolios. These often require students to think reflectively and critically about their choices of artifacts and the rationale behind each choice. It becomes clear that the difference between notebooks or scrapbooks and portfolios is the higher level of thinking, both critically and creatively, that occurs and that is documented.

Typically, when students compile these types of artifacts, they have already either found their poems in digitized formats or typed them into a word processor. It makes sense, then, that a poetry electronic portfolio, or *poetry e-portfolio*, would be as simple to compile and would provide students with practice in employing technology to produce a final product.

E-PORTFOLIOS

Electronic portfolios have many uses and take many forms. In the Grades 6–8 language arts classroom, they can be more easily implemented through the consistent use of technology and a plan for development. The steps in developing a plan and implementing it in your language arts classroom are as follows:

Step 1: Choose a Format

There are two basic options for formatting an electronic portfolio: a *generic tools* format and a *customized systems* approach. Advantages to the generic tools approach are that the author has control over the creative "look and feel" of the portfolio, and that it allows the author to demonstrate his or her technology competency in the development of the e-folio. Simply put, this approach requires the portfolio to be created in the Web template found in a word processor, or as multiple linked slides in presentation software. This link support.obu.edu/office2003/ppt/Linking.pdf will take you to a document that explains how PowerPoint slides can be hyperlinked to other slides within the same PowerPoint presentation, as well as to Word documents and websites. At the end of this chapter, I'll provide you with step-by-step instructions for how to create a Web template.

There are also advantages to the customized systems approach. Customized systems refer to software written exclusively for the development of portfolios. The advantages of this approach include ease in aggregating the data included in the portfolios, and ease of use and evaluation. There are a few free online portfolio generators; however, these programs severely limit student creativity in that they create "cookie cutter" portfolios. Every student's portfolio is exactly like the others', with the exception of the poems included.

Step 2: Choose Your Goals, Objectives, and Standards and Assessment Tools

In developing their e-portfolios, your students will need to be aware of these goals and the standards they are meeting through the development of the portfolio. You may choose to use state or local standards, or the national standards on which this text is based. Whatever your standards, list them, and think about how each possible artifact can meet a particular standard. Plan to communicate these standards to your students during lessons. It's important to focus on assessment at this point, so that you'll know how to communicate the criteria for evaluation to your students, and so that you'll have a clear picture of your focus for this teaching activity.

Step 3: Generate a List of Possible Artifacts

How much freedom will you allow your students in choosing which poems, artwork, and so forth they include in their e-portfolios? Generate a list of the required artifacts. These might include specific types of poems from other poets; original poems from the students themselves; artwork designed using the computer; artwork in other media scanned into a digital format; digital pictures; or audio. What optional artifacts will you allow?

Step 4: Ensure a Higher Level of Thinking

How will you ask students to respond to each artifact? You can organize the portfolio so that each artifact has one written reflection. This reflection can be guided by the standard: "Explain how this artifact shows evidence that this standard was met." Reflections can also be guided by more creative elements: "In a few sentences, reflect on how you developed this artifact and what thinking took place as you developed this artifact." This is the element that sets portfolios apart from scrapbooks and notebooks. Students learn to take responsibility for their own learning, and they reflect on how well they met their goals.

Step 5: Provide Technological Tutoring

How much technological tutoring will your students need? If you plan e-portfolios as a culminating activity for a long unit, you'll be more successful in this element if you plan to teach a little technology with every assignment you do. If you can't make that kind of technological commitment, try implementing e-portfolios by cooperating with your library or technology specialist. Enlist someone else to share the load of teaching the specifics of technology to your students.

USING THE TECHNOLOGY

If you've chosen to have your students use a simple software program to create their electronic portfolios, you can follow these steps for creating a Web page using the template in Microsoft's Word:

1. Open Microsoft Word.
2. Click on the "file" drop-down menu.
3. Click "new," and a new menu pane appears on the right side of your screen.
4. In this pane, locate and click on "templates on My Computer."
5. When the dialog box appears, look all the way over to the top, right side of the dialog box and find "Web pages." (Depending on your version of Word, the Web page template may or may not be located in the far right corner of the dialog box.)
6. Highlight the Web Page Wizard and click "ok." A Web Page Wizard box appears.
7. Click the "next" button in that box.
8. Enter a website title and a location on your computer where your files will be saved. Your computer may automatically save these files in your document files.
9. Select a navigation type. "Separate page" is usually the best choice and is easier to use.

10. The next screen will list the pages currently in the website. Click the "add new blank page" button to add a new page, and highlight a page in the list and click "remove page" to delete a page from the website. To add a page that you have already created to the site, click the "add existing file" button and select the page you want to add.

11. Click the "add template page" to insert a page with a layout. Highlight the choices in the "Web page templates" window to preview the template in the main window. Click "ok" to select a template.

12. Organize your website pages by reordering the pages of the website. Highlight the name of the page that will be moved, and click the "move up" or "move down" button. Click "rename" to rename a page.

13. "Visual theme" allows you to select or reject visual themes for your pages. Select "no visual theme" for a blank page, or check "add a visual theme" and click "browse themes" to select a graphical theme.

14. Click "finish" to create the website. You can now add text, graphics, and audio to your site using simple Word commands with which you are familiar.

When you design lessons that include technology for teaching poetry, be sure to clarify your goals and purposes for the use of technology. Take a look at the International Society for Technology in Education standards for teachers and students to see how you and your students are meeting these standards. Don't forget that some of the other technology tools we've discussed in previous chapters are also applicable to teaching poetry.

Look for ways to include not only the technology tools described here, but also those described in other chapters within this text and those suggested in the Resources section of this text. Technology changes and advances so quickly that it's often difficult to stay on the cutting edge in your classroom, but implementing simple tools will give you and your students a firm foundation in technology and perhaps fuel the fire to learn more about new tools.

Take a few minutes to look through the sites offered in the Resources section of this text. You'll find a sample electronic portfolio created by one of my undergraduate students in an adolescent literature course. The format of her portfolio is similar to one that would be useful in forming a poetry e-portfolio. Examples of this nature are difficult to find, due mostly to the fact that most people mistake simple Web pages for portfolios.

In an upcoming chapter, you'll learn how to create *WebQuests* and how to use them in your classrooms. WebQuests are multimedia lessons built around themes. Building your WebQuest around a theme allows you to locate and include many more resources for building sufficient student background knowledge. Some examples of themes that are conducive to great WebQuests are literature of a particular historical period; folktales; Arthurian legends; sentence structure; and particular genres of literature or modes of writing. As you're working on your assignment for this chapter, I urge you to keep in mind that technology implementation comes more easily and is more successful if you begin with a lesson with which you and your students are already comfortable. Branch out and explore, but build new ideas on those that are already established. Don't be afraid to toss parts of successful lessons to the wind and take a chance on something new!

If you are reading this book as part of a book study group or a professional learning community, you may find it useful to complete the following activity:

Use the information you've learned thus far in all of the chapters, and select one technology tool to integrate into your teaching of poetry. Write a lesson plan that has your students use a technology tool to understand, analyze, create, or otherwise experience poetry. Be sure you consider the purposes for using the technology in your lesson and clarify that in your plans. You may find it useful to include a section in the lesson plan where you explain your purpose for using the technology and where you predict what will happen when you teach this lesson. After you've had a chance to teach the lesson (this is not required for this assignment), you'll probably be quite interested in seeing if your predictions were right.

9

GAINING LANGUAGE WISDOM
FROM ONLINE WRITING LABS

FOCUS QUESTIONS

- What are your current plans for (or experiences with) exploring online writing labs and the mini-lesson structures found there?
- What do you believe about the teaching of grammar and language structure through writing and reading?
- How do you currently explore the advantages of a variety of audiences and of positive feedback on students' knowledge of language structure?
- In evaluating your lesson activities that employ technology to teach language structure, what do you find is your most relied upon technology?

No text, workshop, or presentation of methods for teaching language arts or implementing technology in language arts could be complete without consideration of possibly one of the most controversial topics in language arts: What is the best method for teaching grammar and mechanics? Like all other elements of the language arts, this one presents many variables to consider when choosing the best method of instruction. So the old question surfaces once more: What advances in student learning can be made through diagramming sentences, learning terminology and rules, and filling in the blanks on grammar worksheets? Is it more effective to teach grammar in context, through student writing only?

In this chapter, we'll explore some proposed answers to this question, and then we'll launch into a discussion of how technology can assist you in improving students' understanding of grammar and mechanics. We'll also look at a popular online tool, online writing labs (OWLs), for teaching writers about the importance of good grammar.

Every year there are new scholarly articles by researchers who continue to tell us that practicing skills in textbooks or using worksheets doesn't improve students' knowledge or use of language. The skills fail to transfer when students are expected to put together entire essays. Maxwell and Meiser (2005) give us three reasons for this failure of transfer:

1. The isolated study of language skills has a limited effect on the permanent language knowledge we carry around in our heads.
2. We make choices about language through the context in which we use it; a drill sheet has no context, only unrelated sentences.
3. The "dummy runs" in texts and worksheets are far less complex than the students' own language.

If those factors aren't bad enough, consider the factor of all that time wasted on skill and drill when students could be engaged in real writing, and in dealing with grammar and mechanics in the context of their own personal language composition. Grammar, spelling, and mechanics in the context of students' writing are mandatory and meaningful. Students must learn to use these rules and apply them to their own writing if they wish to communicate their thoughts.

If there is so much research supporting the theory that diagramming sentences, skill and drill worksheets, and an in-depth understanding of grammatical terminology do not make students better writers, why do we continue to teach grammar in the same traditional ways? I suppose the answer to that question depends heavily on how we define *grammar*.

If we mean grammar in the traditional sense, we are speaking of the study of the English language in the same sense as the study of classical Latin or Greek. It's from this type of study that we get our terminology for our English language. This type of study is useful, though perhaps less so to middle grades students than to secondary students who find themselves intrigued by the study of our language, how it came to be, and its functions. Does this mean that students need to learn every single part of speech? Most research suggests that the answer is no. It suggests that rather than teach complete lists of prepositionals, teachers should teach the functions of the prepositional. Questioning how a sentence works and what functions the words have is a significant classroom strategy.

If we take the "grammar" in the question to mean *structural grammar*, then we are talking about a student's ability to recognize the structure of a word. For example, the *–s* suffix belongs to nouns and marks a word as a plural noun, just as sentences typically follow a few particular patterns (subject + verb + indirect object + direct object). By the time students enter the middle grades, they have been successful at speaking and writing their language for many years. Recognizing endings and understanding the flexibility of the English language and the functions of groups of words can help students deal with more sophisticated syntax as their vocabularies grow. By asking students to analyze their own words and sentences, teachers can encourage and empower students, and teach them how much they already know about their language.

If the "grammar" in our posed question is taken to mean the ability to begin with a kernel sentence, one that follows basic sentence structure, and then transform it to mean many different things, then we are speaking of *transitional grammar*.

Karanda is my sister.	= kernel sentence
Is Karanda my sister?	= question
Karanda is not my cousin.	= negative
The book was read by Karanda.	= passive
Karanda, who is my sister, read the book.	= embedded

This type of grammar can be taught by having students combine and "decombine" sentences. This strategy teaches students an increased awareness of syntax, rhetorical effectiveness, and use of punctuation.

If we consider the usefulness of each of these grammars, we can begin with what students who are native speakers of English do know about their language, and positively influence student performance and increase their language flexibility in everyday life. We can teach them that grammar is alive, something we use every day.

The debate rages on, and language arts instruction does not stop to await an answer. So, in the absence of concrete answers, what's a teacher to do? Well, first and foremost, language arts teachers should remain informed about the debate. State and national standards and new plans to assure teacher accountability may indeed push for more grammar instruction than your curriculum now includes. The best policy is to be clear about grammar's inclusion in your teaching plans and the methods you'll use to teach grammar. Each method discussed can be enhanced with the use of the correct technological tool. There are tools readily available to teachers who choose any philosophy or methodology of grammar instruction. In the next chapter, we'll discuss some of those tools.

Most recently, the move in grammar instruction, especially at the middle grades level, has been to teach grammar within the context of student writing. This trend has even had an impact on the way English professors at some colleges and universities teach grammar in their composition courses. This method for teaching grammar and mechanics focuses on the fact that the ability to compose effective sentences doesn't depend on an ability to describe sentences grammatically or linguistically. Rather, this method is based in the belief that most proficient writers use intuitive language skills, developed over time as they compose sentences and use language in real-life situations.

Teaching grammar and mechanics from this pedagogical perspective means that most of the work your students do with grammar occurs during the editing and revising portions of the writing process. Atwell (1998) and some other advocates of a writing workshop approach balance this type of grammar instruction with mini-lessons, or lessons presented at the beginning of a writing workshop session. The topics of these short lessons are chosen by the teacher, after careful consideration, for the strengths and weaknesses of the writers within the class. For example, if the teacher sees a great need to learn about the proper use of commas, he or she may build a mini-lesson on this topic and provide students with daily focus on the correct use of the comma within their writings. In classes where grammar and mechanics instruction is handled in this manner, students learn to use many resources for writing. A grammar textbook may become an often-used resource for looking up the rules of usage, rather than a daily source of drills.

OWLs can provide writing assistance to writers of all ages and levels. These labs are usually built, hosted, and staffed by universities or colleges. Because these labs are online, they offer asynchronous and sometimes also synchronous applications. The information you may find in each OWL site varies. Before choosing a lab for your students' use, you should spend some time online addressing the information found at each site.

Some of these OWLs provide a threaded discussion feature or enable students to directly e-mail a writing tutor employed by the site provider. This opens students' writing and language knowledge to new and different audiences.

The grammar and mechanics resources you'll find in most OWLs are intended to be used for looking up the rules of usage rather than as a source of drills. They are useful, too, for those teachers who choose another approach to teaching grammar.

Having students write stories by filling in the blanks, much like the old printed versions of Mad Libs, is a fun way to incorporate technology into grammar instruction. Documents of this nature can be created using a word processor. There are examples of such games at the Education Place website listed in the Resources section for this chapter. Teachers may choose to assign students to groups, or the students may complete this activity individually. When students have completed their documents, they can e-mail them to other class members, or teachers can post these creations on their class websites. Teachers can have students build pages similar to these on their own, using Microsoft's Word to create a Web page. Students simply open a new Word file and choose "Web page" from the list of templates displayed in the dialog box. By clicking "view" from the top toolbar, and "toolbars" then "Web tools," students can add Web components such as drop-down menus, option buttons, list boxes, and check boxes. These features allow students and teachers to compose documents much like those seen as interactive grammar exercises in many of the popular OWLs. For specific functions of each of these Web tools, please see Microsoft's website.

No matter which methodology you've chosen to teach your students grammar or mechanics, OWLs offer activities and resources for every teacher and every student. Begin by visiting some of the OWLs listed in this chapter's Resources area. In each OWL you'll find a variety of sections, each with a specific focus.

Many OWLs offer assistance not only to student writers, but also to teachers of grammar and composition. Purdue's OWL offers PowerPoint presentations for free download. Teachers can use these presentations for mini-lessons or prescriptively, as students need instruction in each aspect of grammar or composition. Purdue's OWL includes handouts, workshops, and presentations. You and your students can find grammar games, interactive quizzes, and reliable Internet resources.

Different OWLs offer focus on different topics and activities. It may be a good idea to describe to your students the types of activities you would like for them to use in class and online. Have students search for these sites and evaluate them for practical use in class and for dependability. This reinforces to students that some online resources are invaluable when they are expected to compose their work in a word processor. Students quickly learn that they can save time and increase efficiency if they know how to locate resources such as online grammar help, grammar practice, dictionaries, and grammar handbooks. If you currently have a class Web page, your students can contribute ideas for use by all members of the class.

After students have generated a list of useful sites and narrowed it down to a list of only the best, you might have them build an addition to your own class Web page. This will serve as a guide for using the Internet resources for improving composition, and provide your students with input on their class Web page.

There is also the possibility that you may incorporate these resources later into an OWL for your own school or school district. Colleges and universities have complex sites with multiple purposes, but with the help of an entire classroom of writers you could organize, create, and post an OWL for use by your class, school, or district.

We have seen the extensive resources that can be found online for both teachers and students. OWLs provide many of these sources and link out to other sources. Earlier in this chapter, we saw that *grammar* can take on many meanings, and that the technology you choose to use to increase student learning outcomes where grammar and mechanics are concerned directly relates to how you define the teaching of grammar in your own classroom. Take a moment to think about your beliefs on the teaching of grammar. Are your grammar lessons focused on specific elements of structure? Do you teach from a grammar handbook? What is your purpose for using the grammar handbook? Is it a resource? Do you use mini-lessons about grammar topics as needed? Does the main thrust of grammar instruction occur in the editing section of your writing workshops?

No matter what approach you use to teaching grammar and mechanics, there are technology tools to advance your students' understanding and use of their language. If you currently use daily grammar drills, or daily oral language practice, can you find the same resources online? There are online grammar games that would help your students see the fun in language play. With the proper software and instruction, your students can create their own grammar games similar to the old Mad Libs games.

If your focus on grammar is within a writing workshop approach, you can find many resources in some of the best OWLs to assist your students as they visit the editing and revising stages, and you may even have students design their own class Web page that functions as a small classroom OWL.

REFERENCE

Atwell, N. (1998). *In the middle: New understandings about writing, reading and learning with adolescents* (2nd ed.). Upper Montclair, NJ: Boynton/Cook.

Maxwell, R. J., & Meiser, M. J. (2005). *Teaching English in the middle and secondary schools* (4th ed.). Upper Saddle River, NJ: Prentice Hall.

⑩

MUSIC, MOVEMENT, AND LAUGHTER: HOW TECHNOLOGY SUPPORTS CREATIVE AND CRITICAL THINKING IN LANGUAGES

☀ FOCUS QUESTIONS

- In the classroom, how do you believe technology stimulates the areas of the brain that are positively affected by music, movement, and laughter?
- How often do you design activities that incorporate other arts, such as music and drama, into language arts?
- Reflect on positive classroom experiences where technology, music, movement, or laughter were present.
- Do you use WebQuests as technology tools for increased learning outcomes?

COGNITIVE SCIENCE AND TECHNOLOGY

In recent years the field of cognitive science has informed classroom practices and changed what we know, and what we do in order to assist students in learning information and becoming lifelong learners.

Biological scientists have long known and communicated to teachers that the brain sends internal messages. This communication process begins when dendrites receive information and carry electrical impulses through the cell body and down into the axon's terminal. Since the neurons do not actually touch, this electrical impulse must be transformed into a *neurotransmitter*. There are over 100 different neurotransmitters, or messengers, in the human brain. Six of those 100 have a significant effect on attention, learning, and memory: *acetylcholine, dopamine, endorphin, epinephrine, norepinephrine*, and *serotonin*. Let's take a quick look at the role of each of these six neurotransmitters and their impact on learning.

Without acetylcholine, long-term memories could not be formed. It plays a key role in activating the pathways of learning and memory.

Dopamine is often referred to as the "learning neurotransmitter." It has pathways that lead throughout the brain, and it is responsible for producing pleasurable feelings, maintaining focused attention, and controlling voluntary motor movements. The production of this chemical is enhanced when you experience pleasure or exciting activities. Neural pathways associated with rewards are stimulated, and the brain remembers that the experience was enjoyable and learns that it should be repeated.

The peptide neurotransmitter, endorphin, helps stop pain and creates a sense of euphoria. It works together with dopamine and serotonin to create feelings of satisfaction and contentment. Levels of endorphin can be increased in the brain by engaging in exercise, laughter, pleasurable social interaction, music, and appropriate physical touch (Pert, 1999).

Epinephrine, or *adrenaline*, in the brain prepares the body for the "fight or flight" response. In short bursts, it can improve memory and enhance attention. Norepinephrine has a very similar function. Stimulating and challenging activities can increase the brain's levels of norepinephrine, leading to improved focus and concentration.

Serotonin plays an essential role in elevating emotions and self-esteem. It is sometimes called the "good mood messenger."

Knowledge of each of these six neurotransmitters and how they impact learning can assist teachers in finding the right amount of activity and engagement to create meaning and to store concepts in long-term, as opposed to short-term, memory. Three activities have been proven to activate combinations of these six neurotransmitters and positively impact learning: music, movement, and laughter or fun trigger these six important neurotransmitters.

LET THEM HAVE MUSIC

Perhaps you've employed music in past lessons, but opted not to add the technology options. There are multiple advantages to adding a musical element to your lessons, not the least of which is that your middle grades students are very receptive to "their" music. Many middle grades students are willing to bridge the gaps from the familiar rap to the less familiar genres of jazz, blues, or classical music. When implementing music and technology, it is important to remember to make those connections with your students' real-life experiences and background knowledge.

Teachers should use their knowledge of the six neurotransmitters when incorporating technology into their language arts curriculum. In doing so, you're not only incorporating technology because we know that it can improve student learning outcomes, you are ensuring this positive learning outcome advancement through scientifically proven measures.

Technology offers many opportunities to incorporate music, movement, and laughter or fun. If you have successfully employed technology projects in your classes prior to reading this text, what were the elements of the lesson that made the project successful? How did those lessons make use of music, movement, or laughter? Let's take a look at how these elements open the pathways for learning.

Music stimulates the entire brain, but it specifically stimulates the neural pathways for attention. It also causes heightened energy levels and combines thinking and creativity. In previous chapters we have looked at the possibility of pairing music with good literature. Poetry is especially easy to pair with music. Have students write a ballad and then find the musical accompaniment from online sound clips. Or, better yet, have students who are musically inclined create their own sound bites using a computer with recording capabilities. Consider for a moment what research tells us about the addition of music to our curriculum, about connecting the neurotransmitters to classroom practice with technology in mind:

- Music anchors learning and sets learning into long term memory.
- Music impacts metabolism and triggers the release of endorphins. This produces a state of tranquil and accelerated learning.
- Music inspires emotions and enhances long term memory by creating feelings. (Dryden & Vos, 2001)

Incorporate music into your PowerPoint presentations and allow your students to do so. This means they will have mastered one more feature of a software application and they will have learned the importance of music. Teachers often have students create collages or artwork in software applications such as Word or Paint, but they do not often require that students incorporate musical sounds.

Teachers can also have students rewrite popular song lyrics and add the musical accompaniment to the new lyrics. These songs may be presented in PowerPoint or Word documents, or placed on the class website for responses.

GIVE THEM A 60-SECOND STRETCH

Your students need to use technology, right? In order to do so, they must sit still in the computer lab or at the computer monitor to complete their assignments using technology, right? No, absolutely not. We know from brain research that movement enriches the brain and promotes thinking. The cerebellum and midbrain, the regions of the brain that control movement, are linked to the areas of the brain that stimulate cognition. Wouldn't it make sense that students be actively involved in whatever task we ask them to complete? So how do you incorporate technology and movement?

When designing an entire lesson to be taught through the use of WebQuests or curriculum Webs, teachers should carefully consider the activities they ask students to complete. Just because students are asked to use a word processor to complete an activity does not mean that they can't also be asked to interview someone who is an expert on the topic of study. Students can conduct surveys and compile information using software programs such as Word, PowerPoint, and Excel.

Language arts teachers typically employ drama in various ways to assist students in comprehending story lines or character conflicts. Begin with lessons you currently teach that have these elements, and look for methods to enhance the instruction and learning through the implementation of technology. For example, if students currently read *Flowers for Algernon* and then view the film adaptation, design a WebQuest for the unit.

The resources can include information on intelligence, friendship, or any other theme you choose. The tasks you create for the students to complete should require movement. If you have cameras for use in the classroom, have students take still photographs demonstrating various actions in the novel. You could also have students take still pictures demonstrating the emotions of the main character. Using a scanner, scan these photographs into your computer and use them to create a PowerPoint presentation.

When implementing technology, remember that the typical attention span is near 10 minutes. Provide time for students to stretch, and teach them proper posture when sitting at a computer.

Stress to students the importance of movement in order to activate cognition.

LAUGH TILL IT WORKS

Sit a class full of students at computers in the lab and fail to provide instruction. What will you almost immediately see on their screens? Games, jokes, and "world's funniest" images pop up on screens across the lab. Why? For years, the teacher characteristic most preferred by students has been humor. Cognitive science now informs us of how this laughter assists learning:

- Laughter releases endorphins, creating a sense of well-being.
- Laughter enhances students' attention to a subject.
- Laughter increases divergent thinking skills.
- Laughter improves memory.
- Laughter reduces stress and improves concentration.

How can lessons involving technology capitalize on the funny side of learning? When you design lessons that involve Internet activities, look for sites that approach the content with a comical tone when appropriate. Create an entire activity where students write jokes or funny stories based on a particular topic. Most importantly, help students to see the fun in using technology to complete a task. Provide alternative activities and extension activities that allow students to show a humorous side.

While it may be difficult to incorporate music, movement, and fun into every lesson you teach using technology tools, it is much less complicated when you plan to teach a unit using technology. WebQuests and curriculum Webs are two tools for teaching small or large units with technology.

Many instructional strategies and sample lesson plans incorporate these three elements through other arts. You may choose

to research ideas for implementing projects that have students
research, compose, and peer-evaluate performance poetry, choral
readings, reader's theater, poetry slams, or pictorial autobiogra-
phies presented in kiosk format.

WEBQUESTING

WebQuests are inquiry-oriented activities in which some or all
of the information with which students interact comes from the
Internet (Dodge, 1995). These activities are deliberately designed
to make efficient use of the student's time, by providing links and
activities structured to keep the student from wandering aimlessly
around in cyberspace. The purpose for this type of instruction is to
have learners examine a topic deeply, build for transfer, and demonstrate a way of using the new knowledge by creating something
to which others can respond. WebQuests generally incorporate
activities that emphasize higher order thinking.

You will find many teacher-made WebQuests online, some
more reliable and better structured than others. All WebQuests
should have the following elements:

- Introduction: This sets the stage for the study and provides
  background information and a hook.
- Tasks: These tasks must be interesting and doable.
- Information sources: These sources can include both online
  materials and printed texts. The Internet sources in a Web-
  Quest serve as anchors to guide students through cyberspace,
  pulling them continuously back to the focus of the activity.
- Process: The process learners must employ in order to accomplish the task is outlined in a step-by-step manner.
- Evaluation: Information is provided on how the task will be
  evaluated.

- Conclusion: This part of the WebQuest brings the lesson to a close. It gives students an opportunity to reflect on what they have learned through the activities, and it encourages them to extend the experience.

There are many methods for developing WebQuests. Much like the electronic portfolios discussed in chapter 8, WebQuests can be designed by teachers "from the ground up" using Web page development software. There are also online templates available for the construction of WebQuests. Please see the Resources section for this chapter, along with those for chapter 11, for examples of these templates.

If you prefer to build your own WebQuest, you will need to develop a simple Web page and plan to have your school's or your district's server host your site. However you choose to develop your WebQuest, there are a few focus points you should consider carefully. When deciding on the topic for the WebQuest, it is a good idea to begin with a unit you currently teach, one that your students find interesting.

As with all good instruction, the concepts addressed in your WebQuest should be real. That is, topics should concern people or activities in the real word, and should ask students to consider issues in all their fullness, rather than to discover one contrived "right answer." The Internet provides a context that is difficult to find in traditional lessons and texts. It allows us to introduce our students to interesting thematic relationships and juxtapositions that create a complexity that should be the goal of every great WebQuest. Once you decide on a topic and being to design a task for your students to complete, consider the following questions:

- Could this task be completed just as easily without the use of technology?
- Does the task require higher order thinking?

- Does the task identify what students should learn and then provide a broader panorama that allows them to connect what they recognize with new contexts?
- Does the task take advantage of unusual perspectives, or challenging contextualization afforded by the Internet?
- Does the task use the Internet to leverage learning, rather than simply to publish student writing?

It is true that we can create WebQuests simply for the purpose of providing instruction. Students can write short stories without the use of the Internet and WebQuests. If the task you create for your students fails to take advantage of all of the opportunities to collaborate, and to extend and explore ideas found online, then we are simply using technology for the sake of using technology. It is just as simple to add a little extra creativity and effort to use the resources of the Internet and the proper technology tools to implement Web-Quests, so that students learn more through the use of technology.

A second method of designing curriculum through Internet links is by means of *curriculum Webs*. Curriculum Webs have been closely compared to WebQuests, but they differ in many ways. A curriculum Web is a set of interlinked Web pages, designed to provide instruction and support teaching and learning of a curriculum. Somewhat like WebQuests, curriculum Webs have specific components:

- Curriculum plan: This is a fully developed plan that defines the purpose of the curriculum and the purposes of the activities involved.
- Home page: This is the entry point to the curriculum Web.
- Activity pages: These pages describe specific learning activities and lead students to the appropriate resources. Each activity provides structure for learning.
- Teaching guide: This guide contains information any teacher would need in order to teach using the curriculum Web.

- Rubrics or other self-assessment tools: These tools allow students to assess their knowledge and understanding.
- Feedback mechanisms: These may take the form of threaded discussion, blogs, or e-mail communications, but all provide students with a method of communication with the instructor.
- Links: This page usually includes links to external websites that have been carefully chosen to encourage students to extend their learning activities.

Curriculum Webs require more planning and time to design. They are more detailed and may be the best tool for teaching large, more complicated concepts using technology. Because it is created from a curriculum plan, this tool is unique to the plan. There is currently no template for free download available on the Internet. Most curriculum Webs are created using Web page design software. Their appearance is very individualized.

Take some time to look through the sample curriculum Web link listed in the Resources section for this chapter. Notice the difference in the complexity of the design, but keep in mind that this technology tool is the next step once you've become comfortable in creating and using WebQuests to teach.

If you are reading this text as a member of a professional learning community, you may find it useful to complete the following activity. If you are still a little unsure of the technology, you may also find it useful to complete the creation of a WebQuest with a partner. Be sure to remember and apply all you have learning about activating the brain.

If you are a person who would rather compose an essay on paper and then type it into your word processor, then you may be more comfortable actually drawing/writing out your WebQuest. The WebQuest template from Dr. Dodge's site is, in reality, one long Web page with links to each step. You may want to write out your information as you progress through the steps that follow.

Step 1

Your first step in creating a WebQuest is determining your topic. Take the time to explore the WebQuests listed in the Resources section for this chapter before settling on one topic. It may be best to begin with a lesson you've taught previously which had one of the three elements (music, movement, or laughter) we've discussed. Adding the technological component will be somewhat easier if you are already familiar with your topic. There is also an added advantage of using an existing resource list. Browse back through the "favorites" you've created as we explored the Internet.

Once you've decided what you want to teach via WebQuests, you'll need to spend some time exploring the Internet to find great sites. Look through all of the links on each site to determine that all are live, working, appropriate, and updated links. Research indicates that many of the Internet's more useful sites are not found by simply searching the most popular search engines (Google, AltaVista, Yahoo!, etc.). To find these more useful sites you'll need to search newspaper archives, public records online, government documents, and special library holdings.

Step 2

Determine how you will build your WebQuest. If you've chosen to use a template for your first attempt, you'll need to locate a site that supplies templates. Most of these sites also provide information about the types of information to include in each page. These are located in the Resources section for this chapter. If you have a Web page editor (such as FrontPage, Dreamweaver, or Word's Web template) and know how to use it, you may choose to complete your WebQuest without a template. There are no step-by-step guides for this type of software in this text, as these are advanced tools. There are, however, guides for each online through either Macromedia or Microsoft.

Step 3

Organize your resources. Will there be enough computers for all the students? Should this task involve group work (most WebQuests do involve group work), so that students may share computers? If there is a need to organize students into groups, you should remember that WebQuests require the same types of elements for successful cooperative learning that traditional classrooms require. Be sure you account for positive interaction, individual and group accountability, and so on.

Step 4

Write the introduction. Be sure to "hook" your students. Add images, backgrounds, and graphics to increase student motivation and curiosity.

Step 5

Design the task you want students to complete. Here is where "the rubber hits the road." This is the section where you want to create an atmosphere of fun, movement, cooperation, inquiry, and creativity! Good WebQuests ask students to create a project or performance. Few WebQuests resort to traditional composition. You may want to add multimedia elements to this task. Have students employ audio, digital video, photographs, and so forth.

Process

This page will describe the process your students are expected to complete as they create their projects. This is where you direct them to outside links and help them to use the vastness of the information superhighway. Be careful and maybe cautious. Check your links and monitor your students' journeys.

You will find step-by-step directions for using a WebQuest template at carbon.cudenver.edu/%7Edlyoung/menu4.html

REFERENCES

Dodge, B. (1995). WebQuests: A technique for Internet-based learning. *Distance Educator, 1*(2), 10–13.

Dryden, G., & Vos, J. (2001). *The learning revolution: To change the way the world learns (visions of education)*. Auckland, New Zealand: Network Educational Press.

Pert, C. (1999). *Molecules of emotion: Why you feel the way you feel*. New York: Pocket Books.

⓫

USING WEB TOOLS TO INTEGRATE READING, WRITING, SPELLING, AND GRAMMAR

 **FOCUS QUESTIONS**

- What are your primary beliefs about the integration of language arts and the impact of technology on communication and literacy?
- How often do you collaborate with members of your professional learning community to investigate curriculum Webs, WebQuests, and online writing labs to determine the value of integrated instruction in language arts?
- What steps do you use to create a balanced assessment tool? How do you evaluate that tool after use?

In the early chapters of this text and throughout the chapter focus questions, you have been asked to reflect upon your core of teaching beliefs; how those beliefs impact your practice in the classroom; and the changes you are willing to embrace in your teaching. In talking about the integration of all of the language arts, we should again address this core of beliefs. You may already hold to the belief that we, as teachers of English and language arts, should indeed integrate all of the language arts into all of our daily lessons, to the extent possible. You may believe that there is a balance at some point in literacy instruction and a difference between literacy instruction and language arts instruction. Whatever your core of beliefs tell you about teaching language arts, it is, once again, important to remain current about the standards in our field.

The National Board for Professional Teaching Standards (NBPTS; 2001) directly addresses the integration of the language arts in Standard XII: "Accomplished Early Adolescence/English Language Arts teachers integrate learning and learning activities within the English language arts classroom and across the disciplines" (p. 53). They further explain the importance of this standard by referring to integration as the hallmark of accomplished teachers, and they explain that integration encompasses two related concepts.

First, the basic processes involved in language arts, reading, writing, listening, speaking, and viewing are reciprocally reinforcing. This fact is supported by research positing that good readers read like writers and good writers write like readers. Proficient writing increases when teachers present student writers with excellent models from accomplished authors. As students learn to model, they become more critical readers and proficient writers.

Likewise, viewing and interpreting visual forms of communication, including the performing arts, bolsters students' ability to interpret literary symbolism or descriptive detail in writing. Students who listen to oral presentations of dialog learn to intently decipher the intonation of voice that communicates emotions in real conversation and increases student skill in writing effective dialog.

Second, in order to emphasize the importance of the integration of language arts to our students, it is important that we help them see the applications and connections of all of the language arts to their lives outside of the language arts classroom. This can be done by organizing language arts instruction around large themes that branch out to other disciplines, such as math or science. This important step in teaching language arts allows students to see language arts as more than simply another part of the middle school curriculum. They begin to see all of the language arts as tools to enhance learning across the entire curriculum and throughout the remainder of their lives.

These connections are easier to make if you are accustomed to teaching in teams or often employ interdisciplinary units. For example, the language arts teacher may teach the parts of a sentence and their functions, and extend the elements of language arts to assist students in better solving word problems in math by taking cues from the sentence structure. A controversial topic such as pollution can also benefit a language arts classroom, when a teacher presents a topic students care about and one with which they feel a connection or for which they feel a responsibility. These topics often supply the opportunity for language arts teachers to teach students to utilize, read, and present graphs, charts, and other research information.

The NBPTS (2001) also emphasizes the use of technology tools for integrating language arts. According to NBPTS Early Adolescence/English Language Arts Standard XII, "Technologies facilitate the integration and underscore the interdependence of these language processes, and they also facilitate the crossing of disciplinary boundaries" (p. 54).

A WebQuest is the perfect catalyst for instruction as described by NBPTS in this standard. It allows the teacher to present students with multiple pathways to learning through the implementation of technology, to assist in broadening students' perspectives and requiring critical thinking skills to complete the activities described in the Quest. In designing your WebQuest, be sure to capitalize on the many ways technology allows you, the teacher, to present information to students, as well as on the expanded methods for students to interpret and respond to the information provided.

Tasks that require students to synthesize, analyze, compare, contrast, make inferences, and make judgments are the types of tasks that make a WebQuest more productive. Often the tasks in a WebQuest ask students to study a topic carefully from various angles and then to respond in a creative manner. Some WebQuest tasks have students build projects using technology, or conduct and present research.

Before you have decided upon a task, consider how you will assess the learning that must take place for the students to successfully complete the WebQuest. In *Understanding by Design* by Wiggins and McTighe (2003), the authors suggest that you begin by determining what enduring understanding you want your students to have months after they've completed the Web-Quest. What is really worth remembering from the task in your WebQuest?

There are many methods for assessment, but if the assessment doesn't fit the task, its results are invalid. Assessment should be guided by three essential principles: Any form of assessment should promote learning, view multiple sources of information before making final judgment, and provide valid, fair, and reliable information to the student and teacher.

You may find it useful, when planning your assessment piece for your WebQuest, to answer the questions in table 11.1 about your chosen assessment tool.

The first and third questions are fairly simple. We usually know what we want our students to understand and do, and which audience will view the results of the assessment. The more dif-

Table 11.1. Questions about an Assessment Tool

Learning Outcomes	Purpose for Assessment	Assessment Audience
What do I want my students to understand and be able to do?	Why are we assessing and how will this assessment information be used?	For whom are these results intended?

Note: Adapted from McTighe & Ferra, 1995.

ficult question to address, especially when we've implemented technology, is the second question: Why are we assessing? It is dangerously easy to lose focus and assess only the students' use of the technology tool. This may well figure into the complete assessment. But is it the focus of the assessment? Did we integrate all of the language arts into a WebQuest just to have our students use new technology tools, or did we employ the tools of technology to advance the learning outcomes (the language arts learning outcomes) of the students?

Some examples of a few purposes for assessment are listed below. Consider these when you are designing your task and your assessment piece for your WebQuest.

- to focus student attention and effort
- to motivate
- to inform and guide teacher instruction
- to diagnose student strengths and weaknesses
- to communicate learning expectations
- to gauge program effectiveness
- to determine students' declarative knowledge only
- to determine the level of student procedural knowledge
- to determine the level of student conditional knowledge

Once you've determined your audience, your purpose, and your learning outcomes, you'll need to choose a type of assessment. If you've searched the Internet to view some of the better WebQuests, you'll notice a wide array of types of assessment tools. The vast majority of these tools assess a performance or product and require *performance-based assessments*. Performance-based assessments are assessment activities that directly assess students' understanding and proficiency by allowing students to construct a response, create a product, or perform a demonstration to show what they understand and can do. These tasks can be assessed with countless tools.

TRADITIONAL ASSESSMENT TOOLS

Some products can be assessed with traditional *selected response* items. These include multiple-choice questions, true/false statements, or matching options. These assessment tools can be linked to from outside of the Web. The burden here is to find a tool that assesses your learning outcomes. These tools can also be built by the teacher using simple Web page editors or Word documents with "Web elements" inserted into the document.

A second type of assessment, regularly considered a traditional form of assessment, uses *constructed response items*. These items require students to fill in the blanks, provide short answers, label diagrams, or create a visual representation such as a web, concept map, illustration, or matrix.

PRODUCT ASSESSMENTS

Student may generate *products* for assessment. These products should be clearly defined, and students should know the required process and elements before they begin constructing the product. Sample products may include models; digital art exhibits or digital student artwork; video or audio clips of product construction; hyperlinked original stories, plays, or poems; Weblogs; research multimedia presentations; electronic portfolios of student work; and spreadsheets. These products are assessed by teachers but require some assessment tools, such as a rubric, checkbric, or assessment list.

The advantages to products as tasks for WebQuests are multiple. Perhaps the greatest advantage is that when students are given the opportunity to produce authentic products, they become more engaged in and committed to the process of production and learning. These types of tasks and assessments allow students to express their individuality and highlight what students can do.

PERFORMANCES

Students may also be asked to create *performances* in WebQuests. These performances may include dramatic readings, choral readings, debates, or musical composition to accompany hyperlinked compositions or digital artwork. These projects are labor-intensive but motivate and engage students in ways that other types of tasks do not. Performance assessment requirements allow teachers to capitalize on the implementation of music, movement, and laughter discussed in chapter 10.

They also allow teachers to directly observe the application of the desired skills and knowledge. Performance tasks and assessments are authentic because they often replicate actual performances required in the world outside of school.

Performance tasks and product tasks require the teacher to create criteria for judging the student's performance or product. These criteria should be thought out, and communicated to the student along with the task assignment. Both product and performance tasks give the students an opportunity to assess one another, thus once again providing a real audience.

Process-focused tasks and assessments include oral questioning, interviewing others, conferencing with groups, thinking aloud, and observing. Unlike previously discussed tasks and assessments, process-focused tasks allow teachers to "see" the cognitive process of a student. For example, if you use modeling or think-aloud strategies to teach students to read a text, you are using a process-focused task. Students talk their way through the thinking involved in making meaning from a text.

This process is easily enhanced with technology by allowing students to "annotate" digital text with their thoughts. Student thinking can also be documented through Weblogs or learning logs. These types of tasks help students to develop metacognitive skills.

Each type of task and assessment listed in the previous chapter requires a particular type of evaluation. These are sometimes also considered *communication methods* for assessments. In other words, these are methods for providing feedback to the student, groups, or parents.

Selected response items such as multiple-choice, true/false, or matching items usually require an answer key, a scoring template, or a machine scoring system for assessment. These are methods of evaluation, and from these evaluations grades can be calculated and communicated.

Performance-based tasks can be evaluated through the use of rubrics, task-specific guides, rating scales, assessment checklists, checkbrics, or written comments. The method of feedback for these tools varies and can take the form of a narrative report, a numerical score, a letter grade, or a proficiency scale.

Rubrics provide efficiency and validity in evaluating performances or products. These types of products often do not yield a single correct answer or solution, but allow for a wide array of responses. Teachers make evaluative judgments by defining desired criteria for quality.

Rubrics consist of a fixed measurement scale and a list of criteria that describes the characteristics for each point on the scale. When using a rubric, it is a good idea to provide students with a rubric and an example of the product or performance. Rubrics can be *holistic* or *analytic* in nature. Holistic rubrics are intended to provide an overall impression of the elements or quality and the levels of performance in student work. Analytic rubrics are designed to indicate the level of performance of a student's work on two or more separate elements or measures of quality.

A tool less often used than a rubric is the *checkbric*. This tool functions in much the same way as a rubric. The checkbric is a combination of a checklist and a numerical rating system much like a rubric. Checkbrics list or describe required criteria for evaluation and give the rater a numeric scale for rating. These tools are much more student-friendly but do not provide the detailed or explicit criteria found in rubrics or guides.

Table 11.2. Digital Art Critique

Critique tells where the digital artwork was found and the clues used to determine that information.	2
Critique describes what is pictured and any action taking place.	2
Critique describes at least two emotions portrayed in the artwork.	2
Critique includes at least two pieces of information the digital artwork supplies that written words might not.	2
Total points received	

Task-specific scoring guides are designed for use with a specific assessment activity, such as an open-ended question about a particular concept. These contain a fixed scale and descriptive criteria. Task-specific scoring guides are best used for evaluation when they are accompanied by examples of responses for each point on the scale.

Perhaps the most important consideration for this WebQuest creation is that you constantly ask yourself if the technology tools you've chosen to employ truly assist the student in making meaning from the information presented. You should be able to locate examples of places within your WebQuest where students will experience opportunity for movement, music, and laughter or fun.

If you are reading this text as a member of a professional learning community, or have simply chosen to engage in an active reading of the text and complete the suggested activities, you may find it useful to continue in the evaluation of the products you have created thus far.

Once you've completed your first draft of the evaluation page, double-check to see if your evaluation tool adequately addresses the task and the procedure you've asked students to use. Are you evaluating only the final product, or will you also assess the procedure the students use to complete the task?

Now that you have learned about the step-by-step construction of the assessment page for your WebQuest and created a plan for a WebQuest or a complete WebQuest, you should construct an *assessment page.* Considerations for the tasks and assessments are presented here. After exploring multiple assessment generators from the Internet, you should be able to create a rubric, checkbric, or assessment list for evaluating your students' WebQuest task. Once you've completed the assessment tool, share it with your professional learning community for reflection and feedback. As you reflect on your plans and the plans of members of your professional learning community, consider the balance of each component of the language arts in your teaching experience and in your WebQuest plan.

REFERENCES

McTighe, J., & Ferra, S. (1995). Assessing learning in the classroom. *Journal of Quality Learning, 3*, 95–112.
National Board for Professional Teaching Standards. (2001). *Early adolescence/English language arts standards.* Retrieved August 18, 2005, from www.nbpts.org/the_standards/standards_by_cert?ID= 6&x=43&y=8
Wiggins, G., & McTighe, J. (2003). *Understanding by design.* Alexandria, VA: Association for Supervision and Curriculum Development.

12

MAKING MEDIA MATTER

 FOCUS QUESTIONS

- What are your goals for the use of media in the classroom?
- How often and for what purposes do you use media in your professional and personal life?
- How do you employ multimedia presentations in your classroom?
- Are your uses of technology most often to present concepts, or to have students manipulate material and make meaning using technology?

Throughout this text we have worked together to create a community of more literate learners among ourselves, and discussed creating a similar community in our middle grades language arts classrooms. You have viewed various technology tools and basic software applications, some of which include audio, graphics, animations, text, and hypertexts. In addition to discussing how these tools and applications can enhance instruction, every chapter afforded the opportunity to reflect upon and discuss the practicality of changing or enhancing your beliefs about the use of technology in your language arts courses. Perhaps you have discussed how effective teachers of language arts curriculum rely on their understanding of cognitive science and educational psychology to maintain an educational philosophy that remains informed of current educational trends. These teachers create lesson plans that engage students in the content as well as assisting them in employing the tools of technology for improved lifelong learning.

By examining each of the elements of language arts individually, chapters 5–9 revealed some of the intricacies of implementing technology in *all* of the language arts, rather than simply reading and writing. As you move forward in this last chapter, you may choose to integrate these areas using some parts of previous activities. It may be useful to look back through your notes on these chapters, or to review the activities and the answers to the focus questions you completed as you read.

If you chose to complete each of the end-of-chapter assignments for this text, you should have compiled a very useful collection of lesson plans, as well as a dependable list of "favorite" sites you've used in the course of reading this text. You should be able to visualize a common thread running through this text. It may also be useful to personally reflect on how your views have changed as you've completed the text.

MULTIMEDIA

What is meant by *multimedia*? If you search the Internet for a definition, you are likely to find many. By simply using the same word attack skills we teach our students, we can deduce that it literally means "many media." Some of these definitions include different types of media and posit that these media, used in conjunction with each other, constitute multimedia. The most important aspect of any of these definitions is that they all clarify the

computer and the Web as essential delivery tools for these types
of media. Have you ever considered how you use media outside of your
classroom? How often do you go to movie theaters? From the following list of media, which do you think of as media for leisure, and
which as media for classroom purposes?

• television
• radio
• newspapers
• art (e.g., paintings, digital artwork, photographs, sculpture)
• magazines or e-zines
• comics

Using the same list, consider which of these media you would
classify as most closely associated with high culture, and which as
mostly closely associated with popular culture.

Media influences all of our lives, both in our leisure time and in
our professions. Our desires may be influenced by advertisements
that surround us daily. We may seek out media for forms of communication, both in our leisure time and in our professions. Cell
phones, messenger services, and e-mails provide us with multiple
methods of communication and entertainment. Media is all around
us. During the 1980s, Whittle Communications placed televisions
in elementary, middle, and high school classrooms across the nation. The one requirement for keeping these televisions? Allow
students in these schools to watch a student-produced news show
daily.

As a part of some states' curricula, language arts teachers are
responsible for teaching the study of media. Many schools produce literary magazines, and some now produce a different form
of literary magazine, an online literary e-zine. Some schools provide students an elective class in media production. These classes
may be responsible for producing a school-wide news show, or an

online version of the school's literary magazine or the school year-book. Many schools have media classes create a video yearbook. Projects of this nature provide students with learning activities and allow students to become producers. An added benefit is the parental enjoyment of, and perhaps involvement in, a project of this nature.

Whatever form media study may take within your schools or your classrooms, it is an important part of the language arts curriculum. It may be the best hook teachers have for motivating adolescent students, and for assisting them in seeing the connections between the forms of media that influence their lives on a daily basis in their leisure activities, and those that are employed in the context of activities to facilitate learning and language development in school settings. This essential connection promotes lifetime learning among adolescents.

In their own lives, out of school, technology has given adolescents the power to become "producers." They are less likely to passively receive information from media than those in the generation before them. Adolescents today are engaged in and are interacting with their media.

While some adolescents still simply watch television, others are involved in the drama that plays out in virtual-world games online. Their gaming systems can now be connected to the Internet, and their opponents may well be playing from a country other than the United States. They carry their music with them in MP3 players and proficiently use technologies that allow them to manipulate the music or the lyrics. Others create their own music and lyrics and share these creations online or with friends. Video cameras or digital cameras have always been a part of the vast majority of the Nintendo generation's lives. Their years have been documented with digital still cameras and digital videos.

Language arts teachers must exploit these connections between "out of school" uses of media and "in school" uses of media, in order to motivate these students and teach them that language and literacy are integral and essential parts of their daily lives, both in and out of school settings. Doing so helps us make our students active language users. This type of media production has a natural appeal for our middle grades students. It is media production in the service of language enrichment.

STANDARDS-BASED INSTRUCTION

Two sets of standards prepared by the International Society for Technology in Education (ISTE) serve as the basis for guiding and assessing implementation of technology in classrooms and schools. ISTE prepared two sets of National Educational Technology Standards (NETS); one set is for teachers, and the second addresses what students should know and be able to do in regard to technology. This educational organization also supports multimedia project-based learning activities.

Apple Digital Learning Interchange offers suggestions for multimedia integration, as well as excellent lesson-plan ideas aligned with ISTE NETS for teachers or for students. These lessons are broken down into logical parts, so that you may view each section of the chapter and a list of materials needed to replicate the lesson.

Considering all that we've discussed about learning theory throughout this text, let's reflect upon some of the connections between social cognitivist learning theories and the technology tools we've explored.

PERCEPTION AND ATTENTION

Learning begins here, with perception and attention. Neither is automatic nor easy to gain. Perception is constantly strained by changes in the learning environment, and attention may falter if the learner is attempting to attend to multiple stimuli. There are three main principles relevant to perception and attention, and technology addresses all three:

1. Information must be easy to receive. Visual information and aural information should be presented to gain attention. Multimedia pairs these to gain the learner's attention.
2. The position of this information affects the learner's attention and perception. When multimedia presentations are constructed, students must be made aware of their response to elements such as volume, brightness, clarity, etc.
3. Differences and changes attract and maintain attention. Multimedia presentations provide these changes.

If you completed the development of your own WebQuest, it should be a multimedia lesson that capitalizes on changes and visual perceptions to capture students' attention and hold it.

ENCODING

Encoding is the process of transferring information that is perceived and attended to into a format that the brain can understand. One particular theory, *dual coding theory*, suggests that learning is enhanced when complementary information codes are received simultaneously. This means that when multimedia projects present text, speech, drawings, music, animations, and video, information is likely to be more quickly and efficiently encoded by the learner. Your WebQuest task should provide students with background knowledge of your topic through text, speech, drawings, music, animations, and perhaps video, providing students multiple pathways to encoding the information you wish them to remember.

MEMORY AND COMPREHENSION

Once a learner has encoded information so that the brain can process that information, the learner must be able to retrieve it and use it at a later time. Two principles serve as the foundation for almost all methods of enhancing memory:

1. Information must be organized by the learner in a manner that makes sense to the learner.
2. The learner must practice and apply the information in order to enhance memory.

A WebQuest task must provide students with various ways to organize the information that you've decided must be remembered. You may present them with reading logs, graphic organizers, or diagrams, or you may ask them to create organizational charts for concepts. The task should also provide for enough practice of a skill to make the skill more memorable.

Comprehension occurs when information we perceive, encode, and store in memory is integrated into our current knowledge of the world. This means that the information the WebQuest asked students to practice and organize must also be information that students can discuss, apply, classify, manipulate, or teach to other people. Comprehension is increased and evidenced when students are able to apply what is learned in school to their lives outside of school.

ACTIVE LEARNING

One of the advantages of multimedia projects is that they have the capacity to require the learner to act, to do something with the information. Chapter 2 revealed the importance of allowing students to get very involved in the creation of projects, performances, and other classroom activities. When content is online and makes use of multiple media, it is even more important to ensure that students are engaged by the media and engaged in the process of completing the task.

Also in chapter 2, we looked at problem-based learning and inquiry lessons. A WebQuest is the perfect place for such instructional strategies. Remember the chapter on music, movement, and fun? Use the media to incorporate these elements. It may be useful to look at the resources in previous chapters for ideas to enhance your WebQuest. In order to keep students engaged in the activity, a WebQuest should implement all three elements.

MOTIVATION

Malone and Lepper (1987) suggest that four factors increase students' intrinsic motivation: Challenge, curiosity, control, and fantasy are essential to intrinsic motivation. Multimedia technologies offer all four components. Students' *self-efficacy*, their beliefs about their own abilities, heavily impacts their motivation. It is important to approach technology implementation with a cautious eye toward students' self-value. Fortunately, since many adolescents have experiences with technology outside of school, technology implementation in language arts classes provides students with the opportunity to do what they already know. Don't forget to praise them in appropriate ways and encourage exploration of technologies. Other researchers have identified positive effects of technology on motivation in these four ways:

- Students using technology experience increased self-esteem. (Teachers who use technology also experience increased self-esteem.)
- One eight-year study of technology implementation found that absenteeism decreased by almost 50 percent (Dwyer, 1994).

- Students participating in technology projects often are more willing to participate in school learning activities.

ADDRESSING THE STANDARDS

The technology tools you've learned to employ throughout this text and the activities you've explored directly address ISTE's NETS for Students Grades 6–8. The technology tools you've employed in this text address the performance indicators set for teachers and students by ISTE. Please visit www.iste.org to view both technology standards for teachers and technology standards for students. Both sets of standards are addressed through consistent and effective implementation of technology tools.

At this point you know how to write the "hook" for a title page, plan out the background information students will need, decide upon a task, and outline the process by which students will complete the task. You have viewed assessment tools and have the knowledge to choose an appropriate assessment tool for a WebQuest.

All that remains is information for completing a WebQuest. If you've participated in the activities in this text, you may have printed the pages of your WebQuest thus far, and it may be easier to look through them simultaneously and make connections among the various parts. It is essential that you also make these connections while viewing your WebQuest from your students' perspective. Remember to check to be sure that necessary links are still live, and that the sites to which you've asked your students to travel are being maintained and updated.

In order to assess your work before asking students to complete a lesson using the WebQuest, you should follow this link to Bernie Dodge's WebQuest evaluation: webquest.sdsu.edu/webquestrubric .html

Be sure to use the links to the fine points to fine-tune your WebQuest.

The teacher information page of a WebQuest allows other teachers to use your product to teach the same lesson. Please think through your connections to the standards discussed throughout this text. In explaining your thoughts for teaching any lesson, be sure to offer suggestions for extensions and modifications for various grade levels.

As with all changes and implementations to curricula or practice, you should exhibit the characteristics of a reflective practitioner. The National Board for Professional Teaching Standards, in Core Proposition 4, clarifies that "teachers think systematically about their practice and learn from experience."

Participating in a professional learning community provides you a forum in which to discuss your educational beliefs with colleagues, to think them through as you collect lesson plans and ideas for incorporating technology into your classroom. If you don't have the time or resources to organize a professional learning community, it is possible to achieve the same benefits by simply being an active reader of the text with a friend. There are also online book study groups for purposes such as this.

However I chose to find another colleague with whom to share my professional development, one lesson I learned well during my years in middle and high school English/language arts classrooms was that if I didn't truly believe in the changes I made in my practice, my students would never see the benefits of those changes. My own practice evolved as I grew as a teacher. I tried new activities, lessons, and technologies as they emerged. When one worked, I kept it. When one flopped, rather than trashing it, I began a devoted analysis of, and long reflection upon, my approach to implementation.

I looked carefully at my own knowledge of my students, their cognitive growth and capabilities, their emotional development, their moral and social development, and even their physical development. My knowledge of content pedagogy also had to be examined. I knew my content area backward, forward, and inside out, but did I know how to make students think like readers and writers? How could I hook them and share my love of literacy? Perhaps most importantly, I searched for teachers who could assist me in my efforts. Teachers who are willing to take chances with lessons and activities need support! They need to know that other teachers have the same ambition to improve student learning outcomes.

There is some level of urgency regarding our attempts to prepare students for the future—not simply for the next few years, but for the next few decades. The understandings, skills, and dispositions we help to create within our students in middle school may well motivate them to complete high school with high expectations of themselves for higher education. I left the middle school classroom room a few years ago, not because I no longer loved my teaching position or my middle school students, but because I enjoy sharing and learning with practicing teachers.

If you are reading this text as an active member of a professional learning community, or you've simply chosen to be an active reader and complete the activities at the end of each chapter, you will want to add the final component to your WebQuest template or presentation. This time you'll create information for other teachers to use, as you contribute to the community of learners employing technology in their classrooms. The final component of your WebQuest is "teacher information." The subtopics on this page should include the standards addressed in your WebQuest, a description of the target audience, notes and suggestions for teaching the unit, and references and resources. Once you've completed your WebQuest, upload it to the discussion board, read the completed WebQuests of your classmates, and offer suggestions or reflections from your own teaching experiences.

If you've used the template download from the website at San Diego State University, you should have one document to upload. This document is essentially one really long page, containing links to picccs of the page. Simply upload this document as you would any other document. If you chose to create your WebQuest in a Web page generating program, you may need to follow the directions in that particular software package. Both FrontPage and Dreamweaver automatically save all pages in a Web to one folder. If you have used one of these programs, you'll need to upload the entire folder.

REFERENCES

Dwyer, D. (1994). Apple classrooms of tomorrow: What we've learned. *Educational Leadership, 51*, 4–10.

Malone, T. W., & Lepper, M. R. (1987). Making learning fun: A taxonomy of intrinsic motivation for learning. In R. E. Snow & M. J. Farr (Eds.), *Aptitude, learning and instruction: Vol.3. Conative and affective process analysis* (pp. 223–253). Hillsdale, NJ: Erlbaum.

National Board for Professional Teaching Standards. (2002). *What teachers should know and be able to do.* Available at www.nbpts.org.

EXAM QUESTIONS
AND ANSWERS

1. Which function in Internet Explorer allows you to compile an organized listing of websites that you find useful and plan to revisit often?
   a. **the "refresh" function**
      This answer is *incorrect*. The "refresh" function allows you to see the latest edition of a Web page.
   b. **the "favorites" function**
      This answer is *correct*. This function allows you to create an organized list of your "favorite" or most visited sites.
   c. **the "search" function**
      This answer is *incorrect*. The "search" function allows you to search the Internet for Web pages.
   d. **the "history" function**
      This answer is *incorrect*. The "history" function contains a listing of sites previously visited.
2. According to research, what benefits do teachers who use technology to teach young adult literature see among their students?

a. improved social skills, increased extrinsic motivation, and increased levels of knowledge
This answer is *incorrect*. Students do not necessarily improve social skills through the use of technology tools in the teaching of young adult literature.

b. improved intrinsic motivation, increased levels of critical thinking, and more and better student self-assessment
This answer is *correct*. Through the implementation of technology in instruction involving young adult literature, teachers see increases in these three areas.

c. student discipline, students' willingness to speak out in class, and student organization
This answer is *incorrect*. Teachers do not necessarily see improvements in any of these factors through the implementation of technology.

d. students' overall reading levels, students' interest levels, and students' independent reading levels
This answer is *incorrect*. Research has found that the amount of reading students do daily will improve these factors, but technology implementation in the teaching of young adult literature has no discernible connections.

3. When exporting Inspiration outlines or concept maps to PowerPoint, Inspiration automatically exports files as one particular type of document. That type of document is

a. an html document.
This answer is *incorrect*. Hyper Text Markup Language is the language of the Web.

b. a Word document.
This answer is *correct*. Inspiration exports every document as a Word document.

c. a plain text document.
This answer is *incorrect*. Inspiration exports every document as a Word document.

d. a PowerPoint presentation.
This answer is *incorrect*. Inspiration exports every document as a Word document.

Chapter I

4. Which of the following statements best describes the relationship between adolescents' in-school literacies and their out-of-school literacies?

   a. The types of literacy adolescents employ outside of academic settings should never be considered in preparing activities for academic uses of literacy.
   This answer is *incorrect*. The connections between in-school and out-of-school literacy should be considered in activity preparation.

   b. The types of literacy adolescents employ outside of academic settings should be considered for their elements of fun when preparing academic activities to enhance literacy.
   This answer is *incorrect*. These connections should be made because students who see that out-of-school literacy is connected to academic literacy become lifelong learners.

   c. The types of literacy adolescents employ outside of academic settings should always be considered when preparing academic activities to enhance literacy because students who make these connections are more likely to become lifelong learners.
   This answer is *correct*. There are no similarities between the types of literacy adolescents employ outside of academic settings and those they use inside of academic settings.

5. Which of the following is the best definition of *multimedia*?
   a. **graphics, animation, audio, and video presented by a computer**
      This answer is *incorrect*. Computers are simply delivery systems for multimedia and are not the only systems of delivery.
   b. **human–computer interaction**
      This answer is *incorrect*. No mention is made of the elements of multimedia.
   c. **a number of diverse technologies that allow visual and audio media to be combined in new ways for the purpose of communicating, with computers often serving as delivery systems for these media**
      This answer is *correct*. It clarifies the fact that *multimedia* is not synonymous with *computer*, but rather that computers simply serve as delivery systems.
   d. **CD-ROM games or Internet-based programming**
      This answer is *incorrect*. Computers are simply delivery systems for multimedia and are not the only systems of delivery.
6. According to Malone and Lepper (1987), four factors increase students' intrinsic motivation. What are these four factors?
   a. **challenge, sensitivity, attention, and activity**
      This answer is *incorrect*. Curiosity, control, and fantasy are the missing factors.
   b. **perception, motivation, active learning, and comprehension**
      This answer is *incorrect*. These are functions of cognition rather than factors increasing motivation.
   c. **challenge, curiosity, control, and fantasy**
      This answer is *correct*. Multimedia technologies offer all four of these factors.

Chapter 5

7. Which of the following is a good context for inserting sound into a presentation?

a. **when the listeners' attention needs to be refocused to the concepts presented**
This answer is *correct*. Listeners often need refocusing after 10 minutes.

b. **during slides that take a long time to view**
This answer is *incorrect*. Often slides that take a longer time to view are filled with text and should not be disrupted with sound.

c. **during every slide, if a sound seems to relate to the graphic on the slide**
This answer is *incorrect*. Sensory overload takes place after a few slides with sound.

d. **during slides that display large pictures or clip art**
This answer is *incorrect*. Slides that display large graphics need silence, so that the reader can focus his or her attention on the graphic.

8. How can teachers best teach listening skills?

a. **by providing long lectures for students**
This answer is *incorrect*. Students tend to "tune out" during long lectures. For more effective listening during lectures, use lecture and listening guides.

b. **by enforcing "no talking" rules**
This answer is *incorrect*. Students need to be able to express themselves, and this offers opportunities for other students to hone their listening skills.

c. **by providing listening games where students are allowed to speak to one another**
This answer is *correct*. Listening games provide students with an opportunity to listen and respond to one another.

d. **by asking students to prepare presentations for one another**

This answer is *incorrect*. Asking students to prepare presentations for one another doesn't guarantee that they will listen or respond to these presentations.

9. What are the six language arts?
   a. **reading, writing, vocabulary, spelling, grammar, and speech**
      This answer is *incorrect*. Grammar, vocabulary, and spelling are only subdivisions of the six language arts.
   b. **reading, writing, spelling, visual reading, talking, and drawing**
      This answer is *incorrect*. Spelling and drawing are only subdivisions of the six language arts.
   c. **reading, spelling, vocabulary, grammar, mechanics, and speech**
      This answer is *incorrect*. Vocabulary, grammar, and mechanics are only sub-divisions of the six elements.
   d. **reading, writing, listening, talking, visually representing, and viewing**
      This answer is *correct*. These six elements make up the six language arts.

Chapter 6

10. What are the stages in the writing process?
    a. **thinking, composing, and organizing**
       This answer is *incorrect*. This answer is missing an essential element, publishing.
    b. **composing, organizing, and redrafting**
       This answer is *incorrect*. This answer is missing an essential element, publishing.
    c. **prewriting, writing, revising, rewriting, and publishing**
       This answer is *correct*. It includes each element.

11. Which of the following best describes elements of a *process approach* to teaching writing?
   a. Teachers generate topics for students.
   This answer is *incorrect*. This is an example of the *product approach* to teaching writing.
   b. Teacher-corrected papers are central to the teaching effort.
   This answer is *incorrect*. This is an example of the *product approach* to teaching writing.
   c. Writing is self-initiated: Every student has a story to tell.
   This answer is *correct*. It is a characteristic of the *process approach to teaching writing*.
   d. Teachers are the single audience for student writing.
   This answer is *incorrect*. This is an example of the *product approach* to teaching writing.
12. Which of the following best describes elements of a *product approach* to teaching writing?
   a. Writing is self-initiated: Every student has a story to tell.
   This answer is *incorrect*. This is a characteristic of the *process approach* to teaching writing.
   b. Teachers are the single audience for student writing.
   This answer is *correct*. This is an example of the *product approach* to teaching writing.
   c. All modes of writing are respected.
   This answer is *incorrect*. This is an example of the *process approach* to teaching writing.
13. Where is the "draw" toolbar located in the PowerPoint, Word, and Excel programs?
   a. at the top of the screen

This answer is *incorrect*. At the top of the screen is a general toolbar showing basic commands. The "draw" toolbar is located near the bottom of the screen.

b. in a menu at the right side of the document
This answer is *incorrect*. The right menu only appears when toolbars are customized or certain commands are made. The "draw" toolbar is located near the bottom of the screen.

c. at the bottom of the screen
This answer is *correct*. The "draw" toolbar is located near the bottom of the screen.

d. in the left-hand navigation bar
This answer is *incorrect*, as no left-hand navigation bars appear in Word or Excel, and "view" options must be modified to have navigation bars in PowerPoint. The "draw" toolbar is located near the bottom of the screen.

14. How can you find the Paint program that comes with Microsoft Office programs?

    a. by clicking Start, Programs, Paint
    This answer is *incorrect*. Paint is located under "accessories."

    b. by clicking Start, Programs, Accessories, Paint
    This answer is *correct*. Paint is located under "accessories."

    c. by clicking Start, Control Panel, Paint
    This answer is *incorrect*. Paint is located under "accessories."

    d. by clicking Start, Office Documents, Paint
    This answer is *incorrect*. Paint is located under "accessories."

15. What effect does "grouping" have on AutoShapes inserted into a document?

    a. Grouping allows you to work with multiple images as if they were one image.

This answer is *correct*. Grouping does allow the user to work with all selected images as if they were one image.

b. **Grouping allows you to choose images to delete.**
This answer is *incorrect*. Deleting images is done through "delete" or by backspacing. Grouping allows the user to work with all selected images as if they were one image.

c. **Grouping allows you to choose colors for individual images in multiple steps.**
This answer is *incorrect*. Choosing colors for individual images is done though ungrouped images. Grouping allows the user to work with all selected images as if they were one image.

16. If you wanted to prepare a table within a document and have it formatted to appear on a website, what function would you use?

a. **the "add comment" function**
This answer is *incorrect*. The "add comment" function will only allow you to add comments to documents. The "autoformat" function under "tables" allows you to create three different types of Web tables.

b. **the AutoShape function**
This answer is *incorrect*. The AutoShape function allows you to automatically add shapes to a drawing. The "autoformat" function under "tables" allows you to create three different types of Web tables.

c. **the "insert table" function**
This answer is *incorrect*. The "insert table" function allows you to insert a standard table. The "autoformat" function under "tables" allows you to create three different types of Web tables. Auto Format function under "Tables" allows you to create three different web tables.

d. the "autoformat" function

This answer is *correct*. The "autoformat" function under "tables" allows you to create three different types of Web tables.

Chapter 8

17. What command allows you to create a template for a particular poetry format?

a. save as type: Web document

This answer is *incorrect*. This command will save the document so that it can be viewed in a Web browser. The "save as type: template document" command will allow you to access and use the document as a template later.

b. save as type: rich text

This answer is *incorrect*. This command will save the document in a rich text format. The "save as type: template document" command will allow you to access and use the document as a template later.

c. save as type: template document

This answer is *correct*. The "save as type: template document" command will allow you to access and use the document as a template later.

d. save as type: poetry template

This answer is *incorrect*. This command does not exist. The "save as type: template document" command will allow you to access and use the document as a template later.

18. How can students access a document template created by their teacher?

a. by selecting "new document," then "blank document"

This answer is *incorrect*. A blank document has no template qualities.

b. by selecting "new document," then "templates on My Computer"

This answer is *correct*. "New document, templates on My Computer" will reveal any templates created and saved as template documents.

c. by selecting "new document," then "templates on my Web sites"

This answer is *incorrect*. This command will show templates saved to a website created by the author.

d. by selecting "new document," then "templates on Office Online"

This answer is *incorrect*. This command will show templates available for download from Microsoft's website.

19. Which type of software will produce an electronic portfolio?

a. Excel

This answer is *incorrect*. This is a spreadsheet program and will not produce an electronic portfolio.

b. Inspiration

This answer is *incorrect*. This software generates outline and concept maps, but not potential Web pages.

c. Word

This answer is *correct*. Word contains a Web Page Wizard for creating Web pages and electronic portfolios.

d. Outlook Express

This answer is *incorrect*. This software is used for e-mail communications.

20. *Transitional grammar* is

a. the study of the English language in the same sense as the study of classical Latin or Greek.

This answer is *incorrect*. This is the *traditional* study of grammar.

b. the ability to begin with a kernel sentence, one that follows basic sentence structure, and then to transform it to mean many different things.

This answer is *correct*. This is transitional grammar.

    c. **the ability to recognize each part of speech and name its function.**
    This answer is *incorrect*. This is only part of transitional grammar.

    d. **a student's ability to recognize the structure of a word and then determine by the structure of the word the word's function in the language.**
    This answer is *incorrect*. This is the *structural* study of grammar.

21. Structural grammar is

    a. **the study of the English language in the same sense as the study of classical Latin or Greek.**
    This answer is *incorrect*. This is the *traditional* study of grammar.

    b. **the ability to recognize each part of speech and name its function.**
    This answer is *incorrect*. This is part of *transitional* grammar.

    c. **a student's ability to recognize the structure of a word and then determine by the structure of the word the word's function in the language.**
    This answer is *correct*. This is the structural study of grammar.

    d. **the ability to begin with a kernel sentence, one that follows basic sentence structure, and then to transform it to mean many different things.**
    This answer is *incorrect*. This is transitional grammar.

22. What are the elements of a WebQuest?

    a. **introduction, task, evaluation, and conclusion**
    This answer is *incorrect*. The "process" element is missing.

    b. **introduction, process, evaluation, and conclusion**
    This answer is *incorrect*. The "task" element is missing.

    c. **introduction, task, process, evaluation, and conclusion**
    This answer is *correct*.

    d. **introduction, task, process, and evaluation**
    This answer is *incorrect*. The "conclusion" element is missing.

23. What are the elements of a curriculum Web?

    a. **curriculum plan, home page, teaching guide, activity page, assessment tools, feedback mechanisms, and links**
    This answer is *correct*. All elements are included.

    b. **curriculum plan, teaching guide, activity page, feedback mechanisms, and links**
    This answer is *incorrect*. Assessment tools and home page are missing.

    c. **teaching guide, activity page, feedback mechanisms, assessment tools, and links**
    This answer is *incorrect*. Curriculum plan and home page are missing.

    d. **activity page, feedback mechanisms, assessment tools, and links**
    This answer is *incorrect*. Curriculum plan, home page, and teaching guide are missing.

24. Which neurotransmitter is known as the "good mood messenger"?

    a. **dopamine**
    This answer is *incorrect*. Dopamine is referred to as the "learning neurotransmitter."

    b. **serotonin**
    This answer is *correct*. Serotonin creates a general "good mood" within the learner.

    c. **adrenaline**
    This answer is *incorrect*. Adrenaline in the brain prepares the body for the "fight or flight" response.

d. acetylcholine

This answer is *incorrect*. Acetylcholine helps create long-term memories.

Chapter 11

25. Which of the following defines a *holistic rubric*?

    a. a rubric intended to provide an overall impression of the elements of quality and levels of performance in a student's work

    This answer is *correct*. Holistic rubrics provide an overall impression.

    b. a rubric that is global in nature, but focused on a specific feature, such as language use

    This answer is *incorrect*. Holistic rubrics do not provide a focus on any one feature.

    c. a rubric that is designed to indicate a level of performance of the student's work on two or more separate elements of quality

    This answer is *incorrect*. Holistic rubrics do not focus on any one feature.

    d. a rubric that focuses on the process of building the product rather than the product itself

    This answer is *incorrect*. A holistic rubric does not provide a focus on any one feature.

26. Which of the following describes one of the three essential elements of classroom assessment?

    a. Assessment should promote learning.

    This answer is *correct*. One purpose for assessment is to promote learning.

    b. Assessment should yield a numerical score to provide rank to students' work.

    This answer is *incorrect*. All assessment does not require a provision for grading.

  c. **Assessment should focus on one source of information.**
     This answer is *incorrect*. Assessment should use multiple sources of information.
  d. **Assessment should be summative.**
     This answer is *incorrect*. Assessment must be both formative and summative.
27. Which of the following is an example of *process-focused assessments*?
  a. **dramatic readings**
     This answer is *incorrect*. A dramatic reading is an example of a *performance*.
  b. **labeling a diagram**
     This answer is *incorrect*. Labeling a diagram is an example of a *constructed response assessment*.
  c. **think-alouds**
     This answer is *correct*. Think-Alouds provide a focus on the cognitive activities of the student.
  d. **spreadsheets**
     This answer is *incorrect*. A spreadsheet is an example of a constructed response.

GLOSSARY

analytic rubric: A device used to identify and assess components of a finished product.

asynchronous: Refers to events that are not synchronized, or coordinated, in time. The following are considered to be characteristics of asynchronous operations: (1) The interval between transmitting A and B is not the same as between B and C. (2) There exists the ability to initiate a transmission at either end. (3) There exists the ability to store and forward messages. (4) There exists an ability to start the next operation before the current one is completed. (5) Students and teachers/tutors are not communicating online at the same time.

AutoShapes: Shapes available for insertion into a Microsoft Word document. These shapes are automatically formatted for ease of use, but can be manipulated.

blogging: *Blog* is a short term for a Weblog. A *Weblog* is a Web page that serves as a publicly accessible personal journal for an individual. Typically updated daily, blogs often reflect the personality of the author.

browser: A program that allows users to read and navigate among hypertext documents on the World Wide Web. Popular examples include Netscape Navigator and Microsoft Internet Explorer.

conditional knowledge: Knowledge of "when" or "why." Students who know how to define a particular reading strategy, for example, have *declarative knowledge*. Students who know how to use the strategy have *procedural knowledge*. Students who know when, why, or under what circumstances to use a strategy have *conditional knowledge* of the strategy.

curriculum Web: A set of interlinked Web pages designed to support the teaching and learning of a curriculum (Cunningham & Billingsly, 2003).

cut and paste: To duplicate material (by right clicking and then clicking on "cut") and reproduce the same material in another document (by clicking on the desired location for duplication, right clicking, and clicking on "paste").

cyberspace: A term used to describe "space" or resources on a computer network—like the Internet.

declarative knowledge: Knowledge of "what," as opposed to knowledge of "how."

download: To transfer files or data from one computer to another. To *download* means to receive; to *upload* means to transmit.

dragging and dropping: *Dragging* refers to moving an icon or other image on a display screen. To drag an object across a display screen, you usually select the object with a mouse button ("grab" it) and then move the mouse while keeping the mouse button pressed down.

drop-down menu: A menu that appears when the pointer hovers or is held over a single menu item.

electronic portfolio: A purposeful collection of student work demonstrating the student's achievement or growth, as characterized by a strong vision of content, and created in a digital format.

holistic rubric: Used when a quicker, less detailed assessment is desired (as opposed to an *analytic rubric*). The teacher determines to what degree the student performance meets expectations, based on the rubric. The teacher then gives the student a grade within the range for that performance level, based on the quality of the performance within the specific performance level.

host: A computer system that is accessed by a user working at a remote location. Typically, the term is used when there are two computer systems connected by modems and telephone lines. The system that contains the data is called the *host*, while the computer at which the user sits is called the *remote terminal*.

hosting a Web page: To provide the infrastructure for a computer service. For example, there are many companies that host Web servers. This means that they provide the hardware, software, and communications lines required by the server, but the content on the server may be controlled by someone else.

hypertext: Refers to full-text indexing schemes, which are more elaborate, and, ideally, more useful in creating *links* or connections between related subjects or terms. Hypertext allows the user to move from one section to another in the text or a related section of text without having to exit the current document and reenter a new document.

inquiry-based instruction: Teaching that allows students' questions and curiosities to drive curriculum. It begins with gathering information through applying the human senses—seeing, hearing, touching, tasting, and smelling. Inquiry encourages children to question, conduct research for genuine reasons, and make discoveries on their own. The practice changes the teacher into a learner with students, and students become teachers with us. Inquiry teaching asks students to connect previous experience and knowledge to new information. It makes use of multiple ways of knowing and of taking on new perspectives when exploring issues, content, and questions.

Internet: A network of networks, linking computers to computers by speaking the same language.

MP3: The name of the file extension and also the name of the type of file for MPEG, audio layer 3. Layer 3 is one of three coding schemes (layer 1, layer 2, and layer 3) for the compression of audio signals. Layer 3 uses perceptual audio coding and psychoacoustic compression to remove all superfluous information (more specifically, the redundant and irrelevant parts of a sound signal—the stuff the human ear doesn't hear anyway; Weblopedia.com).

multimedia: A presentation that uses many types of media such as audio, animation, still images, text, or video.

online writing lab (OWL): A site where you can gain invaluable suggestions about writing in areas *you* really want to work on, like word choice, commas, or cohesion.

Paint: A simple software application that allows the user to draw images using the mouse. This application is located under "accessories" in basic Office products.

portal: A site on the Internet that offers an assortment of services, such as search engine, news, e-mail, conferencing, electronic shopping, or chat rooms.

problem-based instruction: An instructional method that challenges students to learn how to learn. Students work cooperatively in groups to look for solutions to real-world problems. These problems are used to engage students' curiosity and initiate learning the subject matter. This type of activity prepares students to think critically and analytically, and to find and use appropriate learning resources.

procedural knowledge: Knowledge of "how," as opposed to "what." Students need *declarative knowledge* of a reading strategy before they can possess the procedural knowledge and employ the process.

search engine: A remotely accessible program that allows you to do searches for information on the Internet. There are several types of search engines. Examples include AltaVista, Google, Lycos, and Yahoo!.

software: The programs and data that make the computer hardware function.

synchronous: Refers to events that are synchronized, or coordinated in time. Students and teachers online at the same time in a chat room can chat with one another *synchronously*.

WAV: The format for storing sound in files developed jointly by Microsoft and IBM. Support for WAV files was built into Windows 95, making it the de facto standard for sound on PCs. WAV sound files end with a .wav extension and can be played by nearly all Windows applications that support sound.

WebQuest: An inquiry-oriented activity in which some or all of the information with which students interact comes from the Internet.

REFERENCE

Cunningham, C. A. & Billingsley, M. (2005). *Curriculum webs: A practical guide to weaving the web into teaching and learning*. Boston: Allyn & Bacon.

Dodge, B. (1995). WebQuests: A technique for Internet-based learning. *Distance Educator, 1*(2), 10–13.

RESOURCES AND SUGGESTED READING

CHAPTER I

Resources

The Educator's Guide to Copyright and Fair Use
www.education-world.com/a_curr/curr280.shtml
This link will take you to a publication that explains the fair use and copyright laws as they apply to the Internet.
International Society for Technology in Education
www.iste.org
This link will take you to the official ISTE site. Here you will find links to ISTE's standards for teachers and students, as well as useful lesson plans.
National Council of Teachers of English
www.ncte.org
This link will take you to the official site of NCTE. Here you will find links to NCTE's English language arts (ELA) standards, as well as lesson plans.

International Reading Association
www.reading.org
   This link will take you to the official site of IRA. Here you will find a link to the NCTE ELA standards and lesson plans for language arts.
THE Journal
www.thejournal.com
   This link will take you to an online journal for technology in education. This is one of the most widely read online journals for educational technology. It offers lesson ideas and updates on technology tools, as well as a free subscription to the hard copy of the publication.
techLEARNING
www.techlearning.com
   This link will take you the online publication of techLEARNING. This publication offers updates on technology tools for teachers, links to competitions for students, and lesson plan ideas.

CHAPTER 2

Resources

ReadWriteThink.org
www.readwritethink.org/lessons
   ReadWriteThink provides a list of lesson plans that have been reviewed and are directly aligned with the International Reading Association/ National Council of Teachers of English language arts standards. You may search this collection by grade level or standard strand. One of the best sites for language arts plans!
Education World
www.education-world.com/a_tech/
   Here you'll find Education World's list of lesson plans that incorporate technology into many disciplines.
www.macomb.k12.mi.us/eastdet/Plans/PlanList.htm#Middle
   This website lists lesson plans that incorporate technology into language arts classes. The plans are listed by grade level.
www.cln.org/subjects/english_inst.html
   This website lists more than just lesson plans for the integration of technology into language arts classes. It also provides teachers and stu-

dents with links to valuable information needed to enhance the lesson plans offered.

Baylor Education/Inspiration Template Guide
www.baylor.edu/ElectronicLibrary/support/documentation/ inspiration/TemplateGuide.pdf
This file provides step-by-step guides for the 14 language arts templates found in Inspiration. It includes examples of each type of document.

Action Communities for Teaching Excellence
www.pt3.uh.edu/resources/lessonplans_1.html
Action Communities for Teaching Excellence, provided through the University of Houston's teacher education program, lists language arts lesson plans that effectively integrate technology and active learning.

Inspiration
www.inspiration.com/home.cfm
This is Inspiration's software home page. Go here to download your free 30-day trial.

Edsitement
edsitement.neh.gov/view_lesson_plan.asp?id=281
The Edsitement website is sponsored by the National Endowment for the Humanities and offers excellent lesson plans. These plans do an excellent job of incorporating technology, providing resources, and making the learning active!

An Introduction to Inquiry-Based Learning
www.youthlearn.org/learning/approach/inquiry.asp
This website presents information on inquiry-based learning at the middle school level.

The Graphic Organizer Page
www.graphic.org/brainst.html
This page provides tips for using graphic organizers for brainstorming activities.

Suggested Reading

Rubin, A. Educational technology: Support for inquiry-based learning. Retrieved from ra.terc.edu/publications/TERC_pubs/tech-infusion/ ed_tech/ed_tech_intro.html

This article is relevant to many sections of this book. You may find it easier to navigate if you simply click on the topic within the article that corresponds to the topic discussed in the text. For this chapter, topic 7 of this article is most relevant. Click the link here and then click the link within the article.

CHAPTER 3

Resources

Alex
www.infomotions.com/alex/
Alex is a catalog of electronic texts.
Bibliomania
www.bibliomania.com/
Bibliomania is an online listing of electronic books. This site also includes help and additional resources for both teachers and students.
The Online Books Page
onlinebooks.library.upenn.edu/lists.html
The Online Books Page is a searchable listing of books online. Many links are provided.
Project Gutenberg
www.gutenberg.org
Project Gutenberg is an online library of hypertexts.
www.mrwrightsclass.com/
Here you'll find an example of a class blog.
anvil.gsu.edu/LIterature/
This is a blog for teachers of language arts and technology. While you won't see student work here, you may be interested in reading the thoughts of educators like you.
shakespeare.mit.edu/works.html
This site has the complete works of William Shakespeare online.
EServer Drama Collection
drama.eserver.org/plays/
The English Server's drama collection includes a listing of plays, organized by historical periods, and links to scripts.

EServer Fiction Collection
fiction.eserver.org/
The English Server's fiction collection includes access to works of and about fiction.

Folklore and Mythology Electronic Texts
www.pitt.edu/~dash/folktexts.html

Luminarium
www.luminarium.org/lumina.htm
Luminarium includes online literary texts from medieval times through the 17th century. The site has excellent artwork and organization.

A Hypertextual Pudd'nhead Wilson
www.cyberartsweb.org/cpace/cpace/fiction/lancini/start.html
This site explains the usefulness of literary hypertext through a very effective illustration before you actually get to the literary text. Be patient and read carefully. It's worth it.

The Hands of Mary Jo
www.npatterson.net/sara/index.html
"The Hands of Mary Jo" is a poem by Mary Tall Mountain. This annotated poem is a response to the poem by an eighth grade student. This is an excellent example of one student's reading of and response to literature using technology.

The Lit Café
library.thinkquest.org/17500/
The Lit Café is a student-generated website and winner of a Thinkquest award.

The Westing Heirs
library.thinkquest.org/CR0214945/
The Westing Heirs is a student-generated website and winner of Thinkquest award.

Suggested Reading

Leu, D. J., Jr. (2002, February). Internet workshop: Making time for literacy [Electronic version]. *The Reading Teacher*, 55(5). Retrieved from www.readingonline.org/electronic/elec_index.asp?HREF=/electronic/RT/2-02_Column/index.html

Leu, D. J., & Leu, D. D. (1997). *Teaching with the Internet: Lessons from the classroom.* Norwood, MA: Christopher-Gordon.

Pressley, M. (2001, September). Comprehension instruction: What makes sense now, what might make sense soon. *Reading Online, 5*(2). Retrieved from www.readingonline.org/articles/art_index.asp?HREF=/articles/handbook/pressley/index.html

Rose, D. H., & Meyer, A. (2002). *Teaching every student in the Digital Age: Universal design for learning* [Electronic version]. Retrieved from www.cast.org/teachingeverystudent/ideas/tes/

Swan, K., & Meskill, C. (1996). Using hypermedia in response-based literature classrooms [Electronic version]. *Jounal of Research on Computing in Education.* Retrieved from www.iste.org/inhouse/publications/ll/26/6/51r/supplement/index.cfm?Section=LL_26_6

CHAPTER 4

Resources

www.cdli.ca/CITE/number_the_stars.htm
This is a nice lesson guide and set of teacher resources for Lois Lowry's novel *Number the Stars.*

www.sdcoe.k12.ca.us/score/soto/sototg.html
This is a S.C.O.R.E. literature guide published and maintained by the San Diego County Office of Education. This guide and others found on the SCORE home page are excellent examples of how the combination of literature and technology enhance comprehension!

www.sdcoe.k12.ca.us/score/cy68.html
This is the home page for the San Diego County Office of Education's literature guides for Grades 6–8.

Teachers@Random
www.randomhouse.com/teachers/
This site features Random House children's and young adult novel guides.

Carol Hurst's Children's Literature Site
www.carolhurst.com/
This is Carol Hurst's home page. You will find teacher and student resources here, as well as thematic ideas.

www.globalschoolnet.org/GSH/pr/index.cfm
Global School Network connects schools, students, and teachers around the globe. This page allows you to search for others who may be studying or planning to study common topics.

ProTeacher Community
www.proteacher.net/index.cgi?az=list&forum=reading_books
This is ProTeacher's message board for teachers. You'll find book discussions by teachers like you.

Gaggle.Net
gaggle.net/gen?_template=/templates/gaggle/html/index.jsp
Gaggle.Net offers free student e-mail accounts.

eduscapes.com/reading/bud/index.htm
This page has Eduscape's sample lesson plan for Christopher Paul Curtis's novel *Bud, Not Buddy*. This lesson plan includes every link you'll need to incorporate technology into the lesson plan. This is a good model lesson plan.

The BookHive
www.bookhive.org/
The BookHive offers book guides as well as publishing possibilities for your student authors. There are many clips of stories told by popular storyteller Donna Washington.

Kay E. Vandergrift's Special Interest Page
www.scils.rutgers.edu/~kvander/
Kay E. Vandergrift's Special Interest Page offers information on books and authors, as well as literary criticism.

www.underdown.org/topsites.htm
This site has links to personal websites of authors and illustrators.

projects.edtech.sandi.net/kearny/myhouse/index.htm
This site presents a WebQuest for Sandra Cisneros's *The House on Mango Street*.

IRA/NCTE Standards for the English Language Arts
www.readwritethink.org/standards/index.html
Here you'll find the International Reading Association/National Council of Teachers of English standards for Grades 6–8 language arts.

cnets.iste.org/students/pdf/profile68.pdf
This file presents the International Society for Technology in Education technology standards for students.

Suggested Reading

Bafile, C. (2003, March 12). The concept-mapping classroom. Retrieved from www.education-world.com/a_tech/tech164.shtml This is an Education World article on incorporating Inspiration and Kidspiration into classrooms. This brief article includes many excellent ideas and tips for using the software.

Baron, M. (2000, August). Literature circles/club de lecture. *Reading Online, 4*(2). Retrieved from www.readingonline.org/newliteracies/ lit_index.asp?HREF=action/baron/index.html

Kaplan, J. S. (2005, Winter). Young adult literature in the 21st century: Moving beyond traditional constraints and conventions [Electronic version]. *Alan Review.* Retrieved from findarticles.com/p/articles/mi _qa4063/is_200501/ai_n13486814

Kaywell, J. (Ed). *Adolescent literature as a complement to the classics* (Vols. 1–3). Norwood, MA: Christopher-Gordon.

CHAPTER 5

Resources

edsitement.neh.gov/view_lesson_plan.asp?id=332
Here you'll find a lesson plan on Martin Luther King, Jr. from Edsitement, written and maintained by the National Endowment for the Humanities. This lesson includes all the links you need to incorporate technology into teaching language.

The Voice of King
www.stanford.edu/group/King/popular_requests/voice_of _kingFrame.htm
This is Stanford's collection of audio clips of Martin Luther King, Jr.'s most popular sermons and speeches.

Consumer Electronics Association
www.ce.org/
This site enables roundtable discussions in which students can get together with others from around the world for conferencing and chatting.

Creative Classroom
www.creativeclassroom.com/jf99tech
Creative Classroom offers Web-based chatting.
Rock and Roll Hall of Fame
www.rockhall.com/teacher/sti-lesson-plans/
Rock and Roll Hall of Fame's lesson plan site. Many of these lessons include suggestions for audio. These clips can be found online at other sites.
Epals
www.epals.com/
Epals offers a variety of services, including connecting classrooms for Internet projects and communication.
English Language Listening Library
www.elllo.org/months/weeks/games.htm
English Language Listening Library online offers listening games specifically for limited English proficient students, but these games are also useful in teaching anyone to listen to directions.
Cloze: Listen and Fill in the Blanks
www.manythings.org/el/
This project (formerly known as the English Listening Room) includes simple songs played by RealPlayer. Students listen and fill in the blanks within the lyrics.
Storyline
www.storylineonline.net/
Storyline Online is a Screen Actors Guild site funded by a Verizon Foundation grant. You will find many children's books read aloud by members of the SAG.
literacynet.org/cnnsf/archives.html
This site offers current and past CNN stories through audio and video, as well as various quiz formats to test your listening skills.
Academy of American Poets
www.poets.org/audio.php
Poets.org is published and maintained by the Academy of American Poets. This link takes you to their listening room, where you'll find many audio clips of poets reading their poetry.

The New York Review of Books
www.nybooks.com/audio/
The New York Review of Books offers clips of authors and critics reading excerpts from contemporary works.

Suggested Reading

Ferriter, W. (2005, July 1) Digital dialogue. Retrieved from www .techlearning.com/story/showArticle.php?articleID=164302317

Fryer, W. A. (2005, January 1). Tips for presentations with movies. Retrieved from www.techlearning.com/story/showArticle.php ?articleID=55300753

Gautreau, C. (2004, November 1). How to: PowerPoint e-books. Retrieved from www.techlearning.com/story/showArticle.php?articleID= 51200498

Housley, S. (n.d.). What is podcasting? Retrieved from www.podcasting-tools .com/what-is-podcasting.htm

Solomon, G. (2004, June 15). E-Communications 101. Retrieved from www .techlearning.com/showArticle.php?articleID=21700267&pgno=2

CHAPTER 6

Resources

Thesaurus.com
thesaurus.reference.com/
This site helps students, as well as teachers, find just the right word without leaving the computer.

The Eclectic Writer
www.eclectics.com/writing/writing.html
This site serves serious student writers well, although it was created with adult writers in mind. It contains an extensive list of sites organized by genre and writing tools.

Young Writers' Clubhouse
www.realkids.com/club.shtml
This site offers links to the keys to writing success, student writing competitions, and "meet the authors" sites.

Gloria's Website
www.sasktelwebsite.net/fiss/index.htm
  This website received the 2000 Canadian Regional Presidential Award
  for Reading and Technology from the International Reading Association. It is designed to teach language arts teachers how to implement
  a writing workshop.
The Purdue Online Writing Lab
owl.english.purdue.edu/
  Purdue's online writing lab offers links to lesson plans for writing, presentations, and definitions.
6 Traits of Writing
www.edina.k12.mn.us/concord/teacherlinks/sixtraits/sixtraits
.html
  While this site focuses on elementary students' writing, it offers useful
  activities for middle grades writers as well.

Suggested Reading

Atwell, N. (1998). *In the middle: new understandings about writing,
  reading and learning with adolescents* (2nd ed.). Upper Montclair, NJ:
  Boynton/Cook.
MacArthur, C. A., Graham, S., & Fitzgerald, J. (Eds.). (2005). *Handbook
  or Writing Research*. New York: Guilford Press.
Patterson, N. G. (2000, February 27). Weaving middle school Webs:
  Hypertext in the middle school classroom. Retrieved from english.ttu.
  edu/kairos/5.1/binder.html?coverweb/patterson/home.html
Ratthey-Chavez, G. G., Matsumura, L. C., & Valdes, R. (2004). In-
  vestigating the process approach to writing instruction in urban
  middle schools. *Journal of Adolescent & Adult Literacy, 47*, 462–
  477.
Valmont, W. (2003). *Technology for literacy teaching and learning*. New
  York: Houghton Mifflin.
Weaver, C. (1996). Teaching grammar in the context of writing [Elec-
  tronic version]. *The English Journal*. Retrieved from www.english
  .vt.edu/~grammar/GrammarForTeachers/readings/weaver.html

CHAPTER 7

Resources

The Longman Vocabulary Website
wps.ablongman.com/long_licklider_vocabulary_2/0,6658,282760,00
.html
This site offers many ideas for teaching strategies that build vocabulary. There is a feature that allows your students to develop digital flash cards.
Lingonet
www.lingonet.com/
This site offers freeware for teachers. *Lingonets* are lexical puzzles that promote learning of word groups, much like crossword puzzles.
Kids' Domain downloads
www.kidsdomain.com/down/
This site offers many types of freeware for vocabulary instruction, for both teachers and students. You can download pre-made crossword puzzles or generate your own.
Word Play
www.wolinskyweb.net/word.htm
This Web page offers an entire list of useful sites for teaching vocabulary, using everything from anagrams to wordplay.
Wordsmith.org Anagram Hall of Fame
www.wordsmith.org/anagram/hof.html
This Web page features a list of anagrams and information about using anagrams to teach vocabulary.
Hang2000
www.kidsdomain.com/down/pc/hang2000.html
A traditional hangman game is offered at this Kids' Domain page.
Vocabulary University
www.vocabulary.com/
This site offers thematic instruction in vocabulary through the use of puzzles and games. All grade levels are included.
www.resourceroom.net/comprehension/wordparts/index.asp
Excellent lessons for teaching word parts are found in this section of the Resource Room site. Some are directly related to J.K. Rowling's books.

www.teachingideas.co.uk/ict/usingpaint.htm
This section of the Teaching Ideas site offers student handouts with directions for using the Paint program that comes with Microsoft Windows.
cyber.lenoir.k12.nc.us/khs/croberts/roberts2.html
Here you'll find simple computer art lessons from an art teacher. These use the Paint program.
oregonstate.edu/dept/eli/july2000.html
This excellent Web page, part of the English Language Institute's Technology Tip of the Month series, offers many vocabulary games in the form of freeware. There is also a sample lesson plan for using technology to teach vocabulary.

Suggested Reading

Allen, J. (1999). *Words, words, words: Teaching vocabulary in Grades 4–12*. York, ME: Stenhouse.
Pressley, M. (2001, September). Comprehension instruction: What makes sense now, what might make sense soon. *Reading Online*, 5(2). Retrieved from www.readingonline.org/articles/art_index.asp?HREF=/articles/handbook/pressley/index.html

CHAPTER 8

Resources

PoetryTeachers.com
www.poetryteachers.com/
This site offers lesson plans and ideas for teaching, performing, and writing poems. Some of the lesson plans provide places for easy implementation of technology tools.
KidsBookshelf.com
www.kidsbookshelf.com/
This site offers a place for students to publish their poems.
White Barn Press
www.whitebarnpress.com/
This site provides lesson plan ideas as well as a place for students to publish poetry.

www.aurbach.com/demos.html
This page at the Aurbach & Associates site offers a free demo of electronic portfolio software.

Suggested Reading

Cole, D. J., Ryan, C. W., Kick, F., & Mathies, B. K. (2000). *Portfolios across the curriculum and beyond.* Thousand Oaks, CA: Corwin Press.

Daniels Brown, M. (2002/2006). Electronic portfolios in the K–12 classroom. Retrieved from www.educationworld.com/a_tech/tech/tech111 .shtml

Gibson, D., & Barrett, H. (2003). Directions in electronic portfolio development (ITFORUM Paper No. 66). Retrieved from it.coe.uga .edu/itforum/paper66/paper66.htm

Kimball, M. A. (2003). *The Web portfolio guide: Creating electronic portfolios for the Web.* New York: Longman.

Niguidul, D. (1993, October). The digital portfolio: A richer picture of student performance. Coalition of Essential Schools.

CHAPTER 9

Resources

University of Arkansas at Little Rock Online Writing Lab
ualr.edu/owl/index.html
The online writing lab at UALR offers many grammar exercise and writing resources.

Grammar Bytes!
www.chompchomp.com/menu.htm
Grammar Bytes! is full of games for students and teachers. You can also access grammar handouts on terms, tips, and rules.

WordNet
wordnet.princeton.edu/
This is an online game for teaching students nouns and verbs.

Quia Shared Activities
www.quia.com/shared/eng/
This page has grammar games that can be customized by teachers.

**www.esc.edu/esconline/across_esc/writerscomplex.nsf/whole
shortlinks2/Grammar+Workout+Menu?opendocument**
These Empire State College "Grammar Workouts" include games,
tips, and information on grammar and mechanics.
William Strunk, Jr.'s _Elements of Style_ online
www.bartleby.com/141/
**Jefferson County Schools Language Arts Presentations
jc-schools.net/PPTs-la.html**
Click on "Grades 6–12" and you'll find PowerPoint presentations avail-
able for download.
BrainPOP
www.brainpop.com/english/grammar/partsofspeech/
This site offers some free elements for teaching the parts of speech.
Discovery Education Streaming
**streaming.discoveryeducation.com/index.cfm?unique=DC41E019-
BCD3-F4DA-35C8AD8ECD03789C**
This site offers a free 30-day trial membership to view their extensive
educational video library.
A Right-Brained Writing Prompt from WritingFix
www.writingfix.com/rightbrain/storystartersphrases.htm
These writing prompts teach students to understand and use participial
phrases in writing. WritingFix is sponsored by the Northern Nevada
Writing Project.
Fun Brain Grammar Gorillas
www.funbrain.com/grammar/index.html
The Grammar Gorillas interactive grammar games have students identify parts of speech.
Wacky Web Tales
eduplace.com/tales/
Fill in the blanks to write a wacky Web story. Students are asked to
fill in the blanks with specific parts of speech. This activity is part of
Houghton Mifflin's Education Place site.
eLibs.com
www.elibs.com/
This is the electronic version of the old Mad Libs.
The English Learning Area
www.education.tas.gov.au/english/technology.htm#someapp

This website supplies very useful information on using technology to teach English. It includes information on software for use in teaching language arts and suggestions for implementing technology at all levels.

Capital Community College Guide to Grammar and Writing
grammar.ccc.commnet.edu/grammar/

This guide to grammar and writing was developed by a professor of English at Capital Community College in Hartford, Conneticut. Here you'll find many interactive grammar pages, as well as information on teaching composition.

Suggested Reading

Conner, P. (n.d.). Notes on "Nine Ideas About Language" by Harvey A. Daniels. Retrieved from www.as.wvu.edu/~pconner/Daniels.html These are notes on important information from Daniels's book *Famous Last Words: The American Language Crisis Reconsidered.*

Weaver, C. (1996). *Teaching grammar in context.* Upper Montclair, NJ: Boyton/Cook.

CHAPTER 10

Resources

Geo Team's Our United States
curriculumwebs.com/OurUS/

This is a sample curriculum Web from the authors of the text *Curriculum Webs: A Practical Guide to Weaving the Web into Teaching and Learning.*

WebQuest Templates from San Diego State University
webquest.sdsu.edu/LessonTemplate.html

This page has downloadable WebQuest templates. These require that you have the capability to "unzip" compressed files. Here you will also find directions for completing a WebQuest using a template.

WebQuest Taskonomy
edweb.sdsu.edu/Webquest/taskonomy.html

This is a taxonomy of WebQuest tasks. On this site, Bernie Dodge offers many ideas for developing various tasks for WebQuests.

T-Spider.Net
carbon.cudenver.edu/~dlyoung/menu4.html
 This page presents formats for WebQuests. Again, there are references
 to Dodge's templates and research. This page is also a great tool for
 student viewing, if you think you'd like to have students produce their
 own WebQuests.
projects.edtech.sandi.net/staffdev/tpss99/mywebquest/
 This site offers a format for WebQuests. It follows the template downloadable from the San Diego State University site, also listed in the
 Resources section of this book.
WebQuest Alternative Templates
projects.edtech.sandi.net/staffdev/tpss99/upgrades/
 This page offers a variety of downloadable templates for WebQuests.
TeacherWebQuest Template
teacherweb.com/AK/Appleton/WebQuest/
 TeacherWeb explains each page of a WebQuest and provides examples
 of great pages for each type of page.
HOLES
teacherweb.com/AZ/KofaHighSchool/colmos/
 This is a WebQuest created using the template from TeacherWeb.
 This particular lesson involves Louis Sachar's *Holes.*
teacherweb.com/CA/SaintMary'sCollege-Moraga/MsMcKinley/
 This WebQuest was also created using the template at TeacherWeb.
 This lesson involves a creative writing project.
Witchcraft or Witchhunt?
www.teachtheteachers.org/projects/DJacobs/index.htm
 This is a WebQuest written for a high school language arts class, but it
 is a great example for introduction, hook, and task.
Leaf Identification
www.berksiu.k12.pa.us/webquest/LessWentzel/index.htm
 This WebQuest provides much motion and fun! It sends students out into
 the forests to identify trees. This is an excellent example WebQuest.

Suggested Reading

Chipongain, L. (n.d.). What is brain-based learning? Retrieved from
 www.brainconnection.com/topics/?main=fa/brain-based

Dodge, B. (1995). WebQuests: A technique for Internet-based learning. *Distance Educator, 1*(2), 10–13.

Dodge, B. (2001). Five rules for writing a great WebQuest. *Learning and Leading with Technology, 28*(8), 6–8.

Jensen, E. (1998). *Learning with the body in mind.* San Diego, CA: The Brain Store.

Jensen, E. (2000). *Teaching with the brain in mind.* San Diego, CA: The Brain Store.

March, Tom. *Working the Web for education: Theory and practice on integrating the Web for learning* [Electronic version]. Retrieved from www.ozline.com/learning/theory.html

CHAPTER II

Resources

www.teach-nology.com/web_tools/rubrics/
This page at teAchnology.com provides rubric generators for various activities. Some are ready-made rubrics for reading, writing, speaking, etc. Others allow you to create your own criteria set.

Project Based Learning
pblchecklist.4teachers.org/checklist.shtml
This site provides project based learning checklists for teachers. These checklists are divided by grade level and subject area.

RubiStar
rubistar.4teachers.org/index.php
RubiStar provides customizable rubrics.

Exemplars
www.exemplars.com/
Exemplars provides information on creating rubrics for students' performance, as well as rubric generators.

www.sdcoe.k12.ca.us/score/actbank/trubrics.htm
This page at the S.C.O.R.E. site provides ready-to-use rubrics for language arts activities.

**www.wcusd5.net/attend/jrhs/nickensk/webquest/kids/Picture%20
Thousand%20Words%20Checkbric.htm**
This page provides an excellent example of a checkbric.

Kids Helping Kids WebQuest
www.wcusd5.net/attend/jrhs/nickensk/webquest/kids/index.htm
This WebQuest makes use of all of the elements discussed in chapter 11. Be sure to look carefully at the task and the evaluation tools.

Suggested Reading

Lewin, L., & Shoemaker, B. J. (1998). *Great performances*. Alexandria, VA: Association for Supervision and Curriculum Development.

Wiggins, G., & McTighe, J. (2003). *Understanding by design*. Alexandria, VA: Association for Supervision and Curriculum Development.

CHAPTER 12

Resources

Poetry and E-Motion
edcommunity.apple.com/ali/story.php?itemID=429
Apple Learning Interchange presents examples of multimedia lessons. This particular lesson combines music, movement, and fun!

The Multimedia Project
pblmm.k12.ca.us/ClassExamples/classsites.html
This site holds links to teacher or class websites displaying multimedia projects.

Reflections on the Self
edcommunity.apple.com/ali/story.php?itemID=146
Apple Learning Interchange presents the multimedia project "Reflections on the Self," by middle school language arts students.

African Folktales
edcommunity.apple.com/ali/story.php?itemID=126
Apple Learning Interchange presents middle grades students' multimedia projects about African folktales.

www.usu.edu/sanderso/multinet/definiti.html
This page at the Multimedia on the Internet site provides a glossary.

pblmm.k12.ca.us/PBLGuide/Activities/Activities.html
This page from The Multimedia Project combines activities that are part of a problem-based learning format with multimedia. Students create multimedia projects. This page presents sample ideas for activities. While the page has not been updated since 2002, the ideas are still relevant.

www.youthlearn.org/learning/activities/multimedia/video.asp
This page at the YouthLearn site provides lesson plans for multimedia projects. While these are not directly related to language arts, you can easily use the same types of projects to teach students about literary devices, grammar structures, poetry, drama, etc.

The Amazing Worlds of Roald Dahl
www.rblewis.net/technology/EDU506/WebQuests/wonka/wonka .html
This is an excellent WebQuest on the works of children's author Roald Dahl.

Happily Ever After or Not!
www.rblewis.net/technology/EDU506/WebQuests/cinderella/ everafter.html
This is a Cinderella WebQuest for sixth grade language arts.

The Iditarod Challenge
www.montebello.k12.ca.us/edtech/LAMDA/Iditarod/index.htm
This is an award-winning multimedia project from an elementary class. Parts of this page describe activities that would make excellent Web-Quest activities.

Suggested Reading

International Society for Technology in Education. (2000). National Educational Technology Standards for Students: Connecting curriculum and technology. Washington, DC: Author.

Labbo, L. D. (2004, April). Author's computer chair. *The Reading Teacher, 57*(7), 688–691.

Renard, L. (2005). Teaching the DIG generation. *Educational Leadership, 62*(7), 44.

Semali, L., & Fueyo, J. (2001, December/January). Transmediation as a metaphor for new literacies in multimedia classrooms. *Reading Online,*

5(5). Retrieved from www.readingonline.org/newliteracies/lit_index. asp?HREF=semali2/index.html

Simkins, M., Cole, K., Tavalin, F., & Means, B. (2002). *Increasing student learning through multimedia projects.* Alexandria, VA: Association for Supervision and Curriculum Development.

DATE DUE

Demco, Inc. 38-293